The Future of Work

The Future of Work

How the New Order of Business Will Shape Your Organization, Your Management Style, and Your Life

Thomas W. Malone

Harvard Business School Press
Boston, Massachusetts

For Robert, for Laura,
and especially for Joan

Library of Congress Cataloging-in-Publication Data
Malone, Thomas W.
    The future of work : how the new order of business will shape your organization, your management style, and your life / Thomas W. Malone.
    ISBN 1-59139-125-3 (alk. paper)
      p. cm.
    1. Industrial management. 2. Labor. I. Title.
    HD31.M2867 2003
    650—dc22

                                  2003019554

Contents

Preface

I CAN REMEMBER, back in the winter of 1970, sitting alone in my bedroom on my family's farm in New Mexico, typing essays for college applications on a Remington portable typewriter. I even managed to save one of those essays. Inspired by the idealism of the times and with the grandiose self-confidence of a seventeen-year-old, I wrote that I did not want to "confine myself to a mere job, but should attack some world problem that would challenge all my abilities. I am especially intrigued by the problem of technology outrunning society's ability to adapt to it."

For many people, the aspirations of youth fade away in adulthood. But I've been lucky. The wish I expressed in that essay more than three decades ago—to help solve problems at the intersection of technology and society—has shaped my professional life ever since. And it forms the heart of this book.

Although I knew as early as my freshman year in college that computers were the technology that most fascinated me, it took me considerably longer to figure out the societal problem that would "challenge all my abilities." For a while, I thought it would be education, but in graduate school, at Stanford, I found myself increasingly interested in the complexities of organizing large groups of people—in businesses, in other organizations, and in societies.

I had a friend then who was involved in the antinuclear movement. One day, I accompanied him to a planning meeting for a demonstration that was going to be held at the Diablo Canyon nuclear power plant near Monterey, California. There were about forty or fifty of us sitting on folding chairs in a circle in a big, bare room near the power plant. The group had decided that all decisions should be made by consensus, an egalitarian idea that I found quite attractive.

But as I watched what happened in that room, I was struck by how hard it was for a big group to reach agreement on anything. Everybody had his or her say. Then anyone who had any objections to what anyone else said got a chance to air them. Then people objected to the objections. Only after a very long debate did a tentative consensus begin to take shape. But as soon as that consensus was put into words, new concerns were raised, leading to another round of objections and counterobjections. And on and on and on. I can't even remember, frankly, if we ever did make any decisions.

Here, then, was a well-intentioned process, built on nice, anti-authoritarian values, but a process that worked extremely poorly. There just wasn't enough air time for everyone to listen to everyone else in a large group. As I reflected on the experience, I began to think that it should be possible to say some very precise things about the way groups operate in such circumstances. It should be possible to have something like a physics of organizing that included principles about, for example, the situations in which decision making by consensus is difficult. It might even be possible to express through mathematical equations some basic laws like "the time to reach consensus is proportional to the square of the number of people involved."

Such thoughts slowly merged with my interest in computing, and a field of study came into focus: how groups of people could use new information technologies to organize their work in new ways. To pursue this line of research, I became a professor at the Massachusetts Institute of Technology's Sloan School of Management. Along with some like-minded colleagues, I began to build a body of theory about the physics of organizing—or what we eventually came to call coordination theory.

This was new territory, a field that could both draw on and contribute to many traditional scholarly disciplines, such as economics, organization theory, and computer science. And it could, in turn, help people understand and design many kinds of complex systems, not just human organizations but also markets and computer networks. I was particularly interested in using coordination theory to understand how dramatic changes in some of the basic factors that shape business organizations—such as communication costs—were making new kinds of organizations possible.

Eventually, I started a formal research center at MIT, the Center for Coordination Science. In the late 1990s, I codirected a five-year MIT research initiative—Inventing the Organizations of the 21st Century—that involved more than twenty faculty members and researchers and was sponsored by a dozen leading international corporations.[1]

While we're still a long way from realizing the full potential of coordination theory, I think it's fair to say that my colleagues and I have made some important progress in understanding the factors that shape organizations.[2] I still take pride, for example, in having published an article in 1987—long before most people had even heard of the Internet—that used some of our early research to accurately predict many of the developments in e-business over the following fifteen years: online buying and selling, electronic markets for many kinds of products, more outsourcing of business functions, and the commercial use of intelligent software agents.[3]

A decade later, in 1997, I published another article, "Is 'Empowerment' Just a Fad?"[4] Writing it convinced me of one of the fundamental tenets of this book: that by relentlessly reducing the costs of communication, new information technologies are taking us across a threshold into a place where dramatically more decentralized ways of organizing work become at once possible and desirable.

Even though we hear much talk about decentralized organizations and empowered employees today, my work with business students and managers in hundreds of companies, both big and small, has convinced me that the implications for business are much more profound and far-reaching than most people have realized. We are, it seems, on the verge of a new world of work, in which many organizations will no longer have a center at all—or, more precisely, in which they'll have almost as many "centers" as they have people. Explaining exactly what that means is one of the main thrusts of this book.

My intention is not just to predict the future, however. It is, instead, to help you shape the future. As I realized in writing my college applications, technology creates choices, and the decisions we make will determine just what kind of world we build in the years to come. Making choices that are wise, not just economically efficient, means making choices that are consistent with our deepest values. And that's another meaning of putting people at the center of business—placing human values at the core of our thinking about business.

This book, then, is the product of a seventeen-year-old boy's wish, carried across years of study and shared along the way with many talented colleagues. It was shaped not just by the intellectual lessons I've learned in my work, but also by the personal ones. Managing two major research projects at MIT, consulting for dozens of companies, and spending almost two years on leave as the CEO of a start-up software company have given me deep insights into the difficulties of management and into my own strengths and weaknesses. In some ways, I feel I know much *less* now than I did ten years ago! And perhaps this hard-won ignorance is as important to what I have to say here as anything else.

One other personal experience has also shaped my views about organizations. My wife and I have two charming children. And I now understand, as never before, that the choices all of us make in the coming years will not only affect ourselves but also those who follow us. I can't help but believe that we have an obligation to make those choices as wisely as we can—not just for ourselves, but also for our children, and for their children.

Acknowledgments

I WON'T EVEN TRY to thank here all the people who have contributed to the thinking and work summarized in this book about the past twenty years of my research and teaching. Instead, I'll just list some of the people who have had the most influence on the creation of the book itself.

First, I am indebted to many people who made helpful comments or suggestions about the book. I remember, especially, the following (in alphabetical order): Deborah Ancona, Antonio Argandoña, Jordi Canals (from whom I learned the importance of the phrase "putting people at the center of business"), Michael Fischer, Patrick Flynn, Samuel Gratton, Jonathan Grudin, Robert Halperin, Rob Laubacher (whose long collaboration and always insightful comments influenced many parts of the book), Don Lessard, Michael Mascia, Nancy and Jim McLaren, Murray Metcalfe, Ron Milestone, Craig Murphy (who saved me weeks of work by giving me one excellent reference), Mary Murphy-Hoye, Margi Olson, Wanda Orlikowski, Vivek Puri, Fred Reichheld, José María Rodríguez, John Roney (my first friend, who grew up to become an anthropologist and helped me learn about our first human ancestors), Peter Schwartz, Peter Senge, Sandra Sieber, Brian Subirana, Jeroen de Waal, Peter Weill, JoAnne Yates, and Veronica Yeung.

The following people were especially helpful with developing case examples about their organizations: Dennis Bakke, Iñaki Dorronsoro, the Elfanbaum brothers (Bob, David, and Steve), Rob Oyung, Fabio Rosati, Beerud Sheth, and Jimmy Wales.

Next, I would like to thank the faculty and staff of the MIT Sloan School of Management for providing me with a welcoming, stimulating, and fulfilling professional home for the last two decades. I would also like to thank the faculty and staff of the IESE Business School in Barcelona, Spain, for being magnificent hosts to me during my wonderful sabbatical year (2001–2002), in which much of this book was written.

I would also especially like to thank the students in two of my classes, one at the IESE Business School in spring 2002, and the other at the MIT Sloan School of Management in winter 2003. Both these classes read and reacted to early drafts of this book, and the students gave me numerous written and oral comments on each chapter. It is a rare and amazingly valuable experience for an author to receive, not just four or five reactions to each chapter, but forty or fifty! I am forever grateful to all the students in these classes for their generosity in helping me in this way.

Even though dozens of companies and government agencies over the years have funded research summarized in this book, the following sponsors supported the actual writing of the book and the research most closely related to its contents: the IESE-PwC e-Business Center, the U.S. National Science Foundation (grant number IIS-0085725), Intel Corporation, Fuji Xerox, and the corporate sponsors of the MIT Initiative "Inventing the Organizations of the 21st Century" (AMP, Inc.; British Telecommunications; EDS/A.T. Kearney; Eli Lilly and Co.; LG Electronics, Inc.; McKinsey & Company; National Westminster Bank; Norwegian Business Consortium [Norsk Hydro ASA, Norwegian Confederation of Business and Industry, Telenor, Norwegian School of Management], Siemens Private Communication Systems, Siemens-Nixdorf, and the Union Bank of Switzerland).

My acknowledgments would not be complete without thanking the three administrative assistants who ably helped me during the preparation of this book: Yubettys Baez, Peggy Nagel, and Mónica Trujillo-Bencomo.

I would also like to acknowledge Charles Handy, whose work has influenced my thinking in this book more than is reflected in the actual citations to his publications. In numerous books, articles, and one memorable lunch, he inspired me to talk publicly, not just about new organizational forms, but also about the human values that give them a reason to exist in the first place.

I owe a very special thanks to my agent, Laureen Rowland. This book might well have never been written without her. She tried to convince me to write a book for her when she was an editor, and she finally succeeded after she became an agent. Her advice and support and encouragement were probably even more valuable to me than she knows, as I—a first-time book author—navigated each step along the path of writing this book.

I am also indebted to Jacque Murphy and Hollis Heimbouch, my editors at Harvard Business School Press, and to the peer reviewers they engaged. Together, they helped me prune and focus a huge amount of material into a single book. And Nicholas Carr used his remarkable talents to substantially improve the readability and clarity of this book in the last round of editing.

Finally, I want to thank my wife, Joan, and my children, Robert and Laura, for their patience with all the countless hours I spent writing this book instead of being with them. I will always be grateful for the sacrifices they made.

I

The Coming Revolution

CHAPTER ONE

A Time to Choose

IMAGINE IT'S 1795, and you're a shopkeeper somewhere in Spain. You no longer believe, as the ancient Egyptians did, that your king is literally a god living on earth. But you still believe that he has a divine right to rule over you. You can't imagine any country being governed well without a king who is responsible for the protection and control of his subjects.

You have heard of the strange rebellion in North America in which the British colonists claimed that they could govern themselves without any king at all. You've also heard about the recent bloodshed in France that ended with a group of so-called revolutionaries killing their king, replacing the government, and destroying, almost overnight, so many good things. These events seem to you like profound mistakes, foolhardy experiments that are bound to fail.

It just doesn't make sense to say—as the democratic revolutionaries do—that people can govern themselves. That's a contradiction in terms, like saying that children could raise themselves or farm animals could run a farm. People can try it, you think, but it certainly couldn't work as well as having a wise and just king.

Well, of course, today we know the outcome of those strange democratic experiments. They worked. Really well. Over the past two hundred years, democratic ideas have triumphed in Europe, America, and many other parts of the world. While democratic governments have not been established everywhere, their economic, political, and military successes have far surpassed what almost anyone would have predicted in the late 1700s. And, perhaps more important, our whole way of thinking about society—the role of government, the rights of people, the importance of public opinion—has profoundly changed, even in countries that don't themselves have democratic governments.

Now, we are in the early stages of another revolution—a revolution in business—that may ultimately be as profound as the democratic revolution in government. The new revolution promises to lead to a further transformation in our thinking about control: Where does power come from? Who should wield it? Who is responsible? Once again, the result will be a world in which people have more freedom. A world in which power and control in business are spread more widely than our industrial-age ancestors would have ever thought possible. A world in which more and more people are at the center of their own organizations.

New information technologies make this revolution possible. Dispersed physically but connected by technology, workers are now able, on a scale never before even imaginable, to make their own decisions using information gathered from many other people and places. The real impetus for the transformation in business will not come from the new technologies, however. It will come from our own innate desires—for economic efficiency and flexibility, certainly, but also for noneconomic goals like freedom, personal satisfaction, and fulfillment.

And that leads to one of the main messages of this book: For the first time in history, technologies allow us to gain the economic benefits of large organizations, like economies of scale and knowledge, without giving up the human benefits of small ones, like freedom, creativity, motivation, and flexibility.

This revolution has already begun. We saw its harbingers in the final decades of the twentieth century in talk about empowering workers, outsourcing almost everything, and creating networked, or virtual, corporations. We saw it in the premature—but not entirely unwarranted—enthusiasm for new ways of doing business in the dot-com bubble and in the slogan "The Internet changes everything." We see it all around us today in the increasing choices people have in how and where they work.

But, like the loyal subjects of Spain's King Carlos IV in 1795, most of us don't yet understand how far-reaching these changes may eventually be. We still assume, without even really thinking about it, that someone needs to be responsible and accountable in business. We assume that the managers of well-run companies should always be in control of what's happening. We assume that power should always come from the top of an organization and be delegated down.

This book is about the underlying technological and economic forces that are making such beliefs less useful and less valid. It's about the new ways of organizing work that are becoming possible: what they will look like, where they will happen, where they won't. It's about broadening your view of management, stretching the limits of what you think is possible. And it's about the choices these changes give you—and all of us—to shape a new world.

What Will These New Ways of Organizing Work Look Like?

There are many buzzwords for describing the kinds of organizations this revolution will make more common. *Self-organizing, self-managed, empowered, emergent, democratic, participative, people-centered, swarming,* and *peer-to-peer* are just a few of them.[1] The word I'll use most often in this book to encapsulate all these different terms is a simple and timeless one: *decentralized.*

If you are like many people in business today, when you hear the word *decentralized,* you assume that it just means delegating more power to lower-level managers inside traditional organizations—letting, for instance, divisional vice presidents make product strategy decisions that used to be made by the CEO. But this limited kind of decentralization barely scratches the surface of what's possible. Let's define decentralization as the *participation of people in making the decisions that matter to them.* In this sense, decentralization means roughly the same thing as freedom. From this point of view, decentralization offers a much wider range of possibilities (figure 1-1).

At the far left of the continuum are highly centralized organizations—those in which all important decisions are made by a few high-level decision makers (e.g., traditional military organizations). As you progress along the continuum, from loose hierarchies to democracies to markets, the amount of freedom people have in decision making increases.

As we'll see in chapter 4, some companies today already have *loose hierarchies,* in which considerable decision-making authority is delegated to very low organizational levels. Many management consulting

FIGURE 1-1

The Decentralization Continuum

Organizations can be placed on a continuum based on how much people participate in making decisions that matter to them.

	Centralized → ← Decentralized			
Type of Decision-Making System	**Centralized hierarchies**	**Loose hierarchies**	**Democracies**	**Markets**
Examples	Traditional military organizations	Consulting firms, research universities	Political democracies, corporate shareholder meetings	Free markets, the Internet, internal markets inside firms

firms, for instance, let the individual partners and consultants assigned to a project make almost all its operational decisions. The AES Corporation, one of the world's largest electric power producers, allows its low-level workers to make critical multimillion-dollar decisions about things like acquiring new subsidiaries. In an even more extreme example, one of the most important computer operating systems in the world today—Linux—was written by a loosely coordinated hierarchy of thousands of volunteer programmers all over the world.

When most people think about decentralization, they stop at loose hierarchies. That is, they think of decentralization as the delegation of many decisions to lower levels in hierarchies. But what if power were not delegated to lower levels? What if, instead, it originated there? How much energy and creativity might be unlocked if all the members of an organization felt in control?

The right half of the continuum shows what this more extreme kind of freedom looks like in business. As we'll see in chapter 5, some businesses already act like miniature *democracies,* in which the decisions are made by voting. Many good managers today, for instance, informally poll their employees about key decisions, and some companies have made the formal polling of workers a routine part of their management. In a few cases, such as the Mondragon Cooperative Corporation in Spain, the workers own the company and, therefore, can elect the equivalent of a board of directors and vote on other key issues.

What if companies began to take this notion of democratic decision making even further? What if professional partnerships and other worker-owned businesses allow workers to elect (and fire) their own managers at every level, not just at the top? And what if these employee-owners could vote on any other important question on which they wanted to express their opinion?

The most extreme kind of business freedom occurs in *markets* because, in this kind of organization, no one is bound by a decision to which he or she doesn't agree. In a pure market, for instance, no one "on top" delegates to the different players the decisions about what to buy and sell. Instead, all the individual buyers and sellers make their own mutual agreements, subject only to their own financial constraints, their abilities, and the overall rules of the market.

As we'll see in chapter 6, many companies already use this form of organization by outsourcing activities they used to perform inside—from manufacturing to sales to human resource management. Taken to its limit, outsourcing can render large companies obsolete. Flexible webs of small companies or even temporary combinations of electronically connected freelancers—e-lancers, as I call them—can sometimes do the same things big companies do, but more effectively. Such webs are already common in the film industry, for example, where a producer, a director, actors, cinematographers, and others come together for the purpose of making one movie and then disband and regroup in different combinations to make others.

In other cases, as we'll see in chapter 7, you can enjoy many of the benefits of markets *inside* the boundaries of large companies. For example, some companies are experimenting with internal markets in which employees "buy" and "sell" products and services among themselves; their internal trading becomes another way of allocating resources for the company as a whole. One semiconductor company is considering letting individual salespeople and plant managers trade products with one another in an internal electronic market. This freedom gives the plants immediate and dynamic feedback about which products to make each day, and it helps the salespeople continually fine-tune the prices they offer their customers. Hewlett-Packard is looking at creating an internal labor market to determine which experts on its staff will work on which projects.

To understand why such decentralized approaches to management are likely to happen more often in the future, you need to understand what leads to centralization and decentralization in the first place.

Why Is This Happening?

Many factors affect how and where decisions are made in a business or, for that matter, in any organization. Here are just a few of the most common: Who already has the information needed to make good decisions? Who already has the power to make the decisions, and whom do these people trust to make decisions on their behalf? Who are the potential decision makers, and what are their capabilities and motivations? Within the company and the country, what are the cultural assumptions about what kinds of people should make decisions? The answers to these questions vary widely from situation to situation, and they change for many different reasons. Overall, though, they aren't changing dramatically in any one direction.

There is, however, another crucial factor that affects where decisions are made in businesses, and this factor is changing dramatically almost everywhere. In fact, this same factor has historically been implicated, time after time, in some of the most important changes in where decisions are made—not just in businesses, but in entire societies.

What is this factor?

It's the cost of communication.

Back when the only form of communication was face-to-face conversation, our distant hunting-and-gathering ancestors organized themselves in small, egalitarian, decentralized groups called bands. Over many millennia, as hunting and gathering gave way to agriculture, and as our ancestors learned to communicate over long distances more efficiently—by writing—they were able to form larger and larger societies ruled by kings, emperors, and other central rulers. These new societies had many economic and military advantages over the hunting-and-gathering bands, but their members had to give up some of their freedom—sometimes a great deal of it—to obtain those benefits.

Then, only a few hundred years ago, our ancestors invented a new communication technology, the printing press, which reduced even further the costs of communicating to large numbers of people. This breakthrough allowed people to reverse their millennia-long march toward greater centralization. Soon after the printing press came into wide use, the democratic revolution began. Ordinary people—now much better informed about political matters—came to have more say in their own government than they had had since the hunting-and-gathering days.

Was the declining cost of communication the only factor that caused all these societal changes? Of course not. Each change arose from complex combinations of forces. For instance, our human desires for individual freedom—and for the motivation and flexibility that often accompany individual freedom—were critical. But, as we'll see in chapter 2, the declining costs of communication allowed by new information technologies like writing and printing played a key role in enabling each of these changes. Remarkably, the same underlying factor is implicated in both the rise of kingdoms and the rise of democracies.

Even more remarkably, this same pattern of change appears to be repeating itself now—at a much faster rate—in the history of business organizations. Chapter 3 explains that throughout most of history, up until the 1800s, most businesses were organized as small, local, often family affairs, similar in many ways to the early bands of hunters and gatherers. But by the 1900s, new communication technologies like the telegraph, the telephone, the typewriter, and carbon paper finally provided enough communication capacity to allow businesses to grow and centralize on a large scale, as governments had begun to do many millennia earlier.[2] By taking advantage of economies of scale and knowledge, these large business "kingdoms" achieved an unprecedented level of material prosperity.

As a result of this massive—and successful—move toward centralized business organizations in the twentieth century, many of us still unconsciously associate success in business with bigness and centralization. But to achieve the economic benefits of bigness, many of the individual workers in large companies had to give up some of the freedom and flexibility they had enjoyed in the farms and small businesses of the previous era.

New information technologies can be used to further the trend of the last century—the creation of ever larger and more centralized business kingdoms. And some important business changes in the future will no doubt take that path, as ever larger groups of people are integrated to take advantage of economies of scale or knowledge.

But there is a strong counterforce. Just as new technologies helped spur the rise of democracies, reversing the long trend toward centralization in societies, today's technological advances are beginning to spur a similar reversal in business. With new communication technologies like e-mail, instant messaging, and the Internet, it is now becoming economically feasible—for the first time in history—to give huge numbers of workers the information they need to make more choices for themselves. Today, many more people in business can have the kinds of freedom that used to be common only in small organizations. And that can be very good news for both productivity and quality of life. When people are making their own decisions, for instance, rather than just following orders, they often work harder and show more dedication and more creativity.

Even as they encourage greater freedom, however, these new decentralized businesses can escape the limitations that hampered small, isolated businesses in the past. Because the new organizations have access to the best information available anywhere in the world, they retain many of the advantages of large organizations. If there are economies of scale in parts of their business, for instance, they can find the best suppliers in the world to fulfill their needs for those raw materials and components. They can also find customers all over the world, using electronic reputation systems to establish credibility with them. And if someone on the other side of the globe has figured out how to do a particular activity or process in a better way, the businesses can tap into that person's expertise, too.

This kind of decentralization doesn't work well everywhere. Chapter 8 will discuss some factors that can help you decide whether a specific situation is ripe for decentralization. If, for example, you have a strong need for economies of scale or rapid decision making, you might not want to abandon your centralized structure. But in all the places where qualities like motivation, flexibility, and creativity are important to a business—and that's *lots* of places—decentralization will become increasingly desirable in the coming decades. Centralized management isn't going away, but its market share is likely to decrease.

Even where decentralization is desirable, however, the changes won't all happen overnight. Just as the democratic transformation of societies evolved in fits and starts over many decades, the changes in business will take many years to play out. And every time there is a setback in one place, or a failure to move forward somewhere else, some people will say that things aren't going to change after all. When managers overinvested in e-business, and the speculative new-economy bubble burst, many assumed that the old economy had won and that we were going back to business as usual.

But the relentless declines in the cost of communication mean that there will be ever more opportunities for decentralization. The fundamental changes in the economics of communication and decision making will continue working their way through the economy, company after company, industry after industry, for many, many years to come.

What Does This Mean for You?

If decentralization becomes increasingly desirable in business, then we will need to manage in new ways. But most of us still have—deep in our minds—models of management based on the classic, centralized philosophy of command and control. To be successful in the world we're entering, we will need a new set of mental models. While these new models should not exclude the possibility of commanding and controlling, they need to encompass a much wider range of possibilities—both centralized and decentralized.

Here is one way of summarizing this new perspective: We need to shift our thinking from command-and-control to coordinate-and-cultivate. As chapter 9 explains, when you *coordinate,* you organize work so that good things happen, whether you are in control or not. Some kinds of coordination are centralized; others are decentralized. But either way, coordination focuses on the activities that need to be accomplished and the relationships among them. We'll see, for instance, how looking at the "deep structure" of business activities can help you think of innovative new ways to coordinate them. We'll also see how rigid standards in one part of a business system can sometimes—paradoxically—allow much more flexibility and freedom in other parts of the same system.

Chapter 10 describes how *cultivation* can help you tailor your managerial approach to the situation at hand. Sometimes, you need to give people direct commands; other times, you just need to help them develop their own natural strengths. Good cultivation involves finding the right balance between centralized and decentralized management, between controlling and letting go. For instance, developing your capabilities for visioning, sense-making, relating, and inventing can help you exercise effective leadership from wherever you are in an organization—the top, the bottom, or anywhere in between. We'll also see how—again paradoxically—the best way to gain power is sometimes to give it away.

Coordinating and cultivating are not the opposites of commanding and controlling; they are the supersets. That is, they include the whole range of possibilities for management, from the completely centralized to the completely decentralized.

And therein lies another key message of this book: To be an effective manager in the world we're entering, you can't be stuck in a centralized mind-set.[3] You need to be able to move flexibly back and forth on the decentralization continuum. Since most of us already understand centralization, what we need to understand better is decentralization. And this will be the main focus of the pages that follow.

One other theme runs through the whole book: human values. If more people have more freedom in business, they will naturally seek the things they value—and different people value different things. We'll need, therefore, to broaden our thinking about business. We'll need to expand beyond our narrow goal of maximizing the economic interests of investors to include more of the things that matter to investors as people. And we'll need to think about the various values of workers, customers, suppliers, and others, too. Surprisingly, one of the best ways to reconcile all these different human desires may be the use of the most decentralized decision-making mechanism of all—a marketplace for values. Explaining what this means for businesses and for you will be the focus of chapter 11.

The Choices

Like the democratic revolution that preceded it, today's business revolution will bring dramatic changes in the economies, the organizations, and the cultural assumptions of our society. And, as in any time of dramatic change, small choices will often have big effects. Whether you participate in events as significant as writing the American Declaration of Independence or whether you just make frequent daily decisions about what work to do and how to do it, you will be shaping the world in which we and our descendants will live for the rest of this century.

If you choose to, you can use the possibilities opened up by information technology to help create a world that is both more economically efficient and more flexible than has ever before been possible. But that isn't the end of the possibilities these new technologies provide. Because you will have more choices, you'll be able to bring more of your own values into business. And that means you can put a broader range of your values, not just the economic ones, at the center of your thinking about business.

In other words, you can—if you choose—use your work to help create a world that is not just richer, but better.

An Amazing Pattern

MORE THAN SEVENTY YEARS AGO, my grandfather started farming a plot of land in New Mexico. My father farmed there, too, living and working on the same farm for almost his entire life. As a small business owner, my father had a lot of choices about what to do and when to do it, but he worked long hours almost every day of the week. Although he often did physical tasks, like driving tractors and feeding cattle, he also talked frequently to the handful of hired laborers who worked on the farm and to his father and brother, who were its co-owners. From time to time, he also talked to suppliers (of necessities like fertilizer and farm equipment), to buyers (of the crops and livestock he produced), and to other farmers, but these outside conversations took up only a small part of his day. As I grew up, I sometimes worked on the farm myself, irrigating the cotton and alfalfa, helping feed the sheep and cattle, raising lambs in our backyard for a couple of years. Until I was about thirteen years old, we had an old-fashioned hand-cranked telephone. I didn't even see a computer until I was about fourteen. I think it's fair to say that I know the agrarian life firsthand.

But, like countless others in the generations before mine, I chose to leave that way of life and move to the city. Many of my predecessors went from a farm to a factory, but I skipped that step altogether. Instead, I became a professor at a university. Even though professors, in some form, have existed for ages, my work as a professor today—as a researcher, teacher, and consultant—embodies many of the characteristics of a postindustrial job: I have a huge amount of freedom in deciding what work to do and when and where to do it. Knowledge, creativity, and motivation are critical to my success. I work with constantly shifting networks of people from all over the world, and much of my life is spent communicating with others, whether in meetings, by telephone, or via e-mail.

In a sense, my own life has moved from the agricultural past to the postindustrial future. It thus embodies the trajectory that business organizations have followed over the last two hundred years or so. But that trajectory itself echoes a much larger pattern. To an amazing degree, the recent evolution in business organizations follows the pattern of evolution in the organization of societies. And to understand that pattern, we need to start a long, long time ago—back at the very beginnings of humanity.

The Pattern in Human Societies

Two million years ago, some of the earliest protohumans lived on the plains of Africa.[1] Like many of their animal ancestors, they supported themselves by hunting wild animals and gathering wild plants. Gradually, these early humans spread around the globe, evolving, by about 100,000 years ago, into biologically modern humans.[2] Figure 2-1 shows—in highly simplified form—the sequence of changes that have occurred in the organization of societies since the dawn of humankind. From living as isolated, decentralized bands of hunter-gatherers, our ancestors slowly formed larger and larger centralized kingdoms.

FIGURE 2-1

The major ways human societies have been organized throughout history reveal a remarkably simple pattern that foreshadows how businesses are now changing.

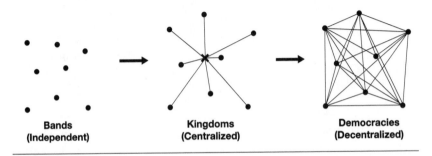

| **Bands** (Independent) | **Kingdoms** (Centralized) | **Democracies** (Decentralized) |

Then, in many cases, they eventually established more decentralized democracies.

What could explain this pattern? Why did large, centralized kingdoms virtually always follow the spread of agriculture? Why were there no large-scale democracies for thousands of years, and then within only two hundred years, the vast majority of countries in the developed world became democracies?

Many factors influenced these changes, of course. But to a degree that few appreciate, a single factor—the declining costs of communication—made the changes possible. And at each step along the way, our ancestors' values played a key role in the organizational choices they made.

To see how communication costs and human values can explain so much, let's consider each of the two major transitions in turn: from bands to kingdoms and from kingdoms to democracies.

From Bands to Kingdoms:
Farming, Chiefs, and the Rise of Centralization

For almost all of human history—until about 12,000 years ago—people survived by hunting and gathering.[3] Hunter-gatherers usually lived in small groups of between fifteen and fifty people, which anthropologists call *bands*. As figure 2-1 shows, the bands were largely independent, unconnected from one another. But within each band there were tight connections, with a great deal of communication between members. There weren't big differences in power and status among members, and most people participated directly in the band's egalitarian decision making.[4]

Here is how anthropologist Richard Lee describes the !Kung San* people of Africa, a hunter-gatherer society that remained isolated from civilization until the mid-1960s and was then extensively studied: "In egalitarian societies such as the !Kung's, group activities unfold, plans

---

*The exclamation point in *!Kung* is the symbol that linguists use to represent a clicking sound in the language of these people. The sound has no natural correspondence to any letter in the Roman alphabet.

are made, and decisions are arrived at—all apparently without a clear focus of authority or influence. . . . In group discussions, [some] people may speak out more than others, may be deferred to by others, and one gets the feeling that their opinions hold a bit more weight than the opinions of other discussants. Whatever their skills, !Kung leaders have no formal authority. They can only persuade, but never enforce their will on others."[5]

When Lee asked a !Kung elder about local leaders, or "headmen," the elder replied, "Of course we have headmen! . . . In fact, we are all headmen. . . . Each one of us is headman over himself!"[6] Indeed, if any member of the group felt that his autonomy had been unduly curtailed, he was free to leave to join another band.[7]

For tens of thousands of years, all people lived some version of this hunting-and-gathering lifestyle.[8] But, little by little, things began to change. Gradually, probably starting about 10,000 B.C., people in the Fertile Crescent, the rich agricultural land of the Middle East, began to systematically cultivate plants and raise animals for their food instead of relying solely on hunting and gathering.[9]

As agriculture spread and population densities increased, larger, more centralized, and more hierarchical forms of organization inevitably followed. Rulers came into power—kings, chiefs, or emperors—and they and their representatives made many key decisions. Hierarchical communication systems were established to support the centralized decision making.

For example, the Sumerians, a society that thrived in the area of modern-day Iraq during the third and fourth millennia B.C., were one of the first to invent farming. Not coincidentally, they were probably also the first to use a word (*lu-gal,* or "great man") to mean "king." In the Sumerian kingdom, as in many monarchies throughout history, kings had immense power over the lives of their subjects and were often thought to be gods. Even in monarchical societies in which kings were not considered literal gods, people commonly believed—as reflected in the European doctrine of the divine right of kings—that the king's authority came from God and that the king was the source and center of all political power.[10]

The increasing centralization of societies did not unfold without disruptions, of course. Kings and kingdoms came and went, and all the great empires—Roman, Egyptian, Chinese, Arab, Aztec, Inca—

eventually broke apart. But each time, new kings or emperors arose and took power, often forming even bigger and more centralized kingdoms than before. With just a few isolated exceptions (most notably the Greek democracies around 400 B.C.), the trend of increasing centralization continued for thousands of years, coming to an end only a few centuries ago.

It's worth pausing to sum up what we've just seen: As humans advanced from the hunter-gatherer stage to agriculture, their organized groups inevitably became both larger and more centralized.[11] We usually take this fact for granted today, yet it is one of the most consistent and—in some ways—most surprising findings to emerge from the study of organizational history. Why did it happen? Humans changed the way they organized themselves, because falling communication costs made the changes *possible,* and people's values made the changes *desirable.*

Falling Communication Costs Made Bigger Organizations Possible

The only way our hunter-gatherer ancestors could communicate with one another was face-to-face. And because wild food supplies were limited, their bands usually had to live relatively far apart to have enough to eat. Therefore, they often had to travel long distances just to be able to exchange even the simplest information with members of other bands. Farming allowed people to live closer together however, so over time these communication costs fell. The lower cost of communication, in turn, enabled the first stage in the development of larger organizations. But there were still significant limits on how many people could live closely enough together to communicate effectively.

These limits diminished significantly sometime around 3,000 B.C., when humanity made another profoundly important invention: the technology of writing. For the first time, people could communicate with each other over long distances without ever meeting face-to-face.

Many people regard writing as the key distinction between civilization and all other forms of human society.[12] More technically, civilization is often defined as involving *state-level societies,* that is, societies that have developed large, complex, multilevel organizations. While there is no consensus among anthropologists about all the factors that cause states to emerge, writing is almost always an essential ingredient.[13] Without writing, it is virtually impossible to administer a large and complex state.

Bigger Organizations Gave People Things They Wanted

Falling communication costs made bigger organizations possible, but they did not make big organizations necessary. In principle, the early farmers could have followed the organizational model of their hunter-gatherer predecessors and continued working in small, independent bands of about twenty-five people—sharing the work, sharing information about farming, sharing food in times of troubles, and occasionally fighting together against other bands. Each band might have remained autonomous and egalitarian, eschewing any strong central leader.

But that didn't happen. Larger groups must have offered clear advantages over smaller ones. In retrospect, we can see two obvious advantages: Larger groups were better at producing food and other "economic" goods, and they were better at fighting.

Economic Advantages of Large Organizations   Larger groups offer greater opportunities for economies of scale and specialization of labor. For example, we can see the benefits of specialization by looking at the early societies of the Pacific Northwest (what is now Washington, Oregon, and British Columbia). This area was unusually rich in fish and game—one early explorer said that the salmon in the rivers were so dense "you could walk across their backs."[14] The rich resources allowed hunters and gatherers to settle the coast much more densely than was common elsewhere. The large settlements of these people thus provide a valuable example of a transitional kind of economic structure. In these societies, all families had to hunt and gather, but many families also had sideline specialties, like making fishhooks or bear traps.[15] The Nootka, for example, had a wide array of fishhooks, ranging from heat-treated spruce hooks for halibut to bone hooks for cod. Nootka boats ranged from one-man canoes to sixty-foot cargo boats. Moreover, the hunters used different kinds of traps for bear, deer, elk, and salmon.

Of course, with all this specialization, some way of redistributing the resulting products was needed. The fishhook makers sometimes needed boats, and the boat makers sometimes needed fishhooks. A political leader, or "Big Man," in each village provided this redistribution function. The Big Man made sure that there were enough people specializing in each craft. He coordinated the sharing of specialized products and even arranged for trading with other villages. In compensation, he took as much as one-half of a hunter's kill or a fisher's haul. Some of this he returned directly to people through public feasts, but some of it—not surprisingly—he kept for himself.[16]

Military Advantages of Large Organizations It hardly needs saying that for most forms of traditional warfare, size is a significant advantage. As Jared Diamond puts it, "ten malnourished farmers can still outfight one healthy hunter."[17] But why should ten or one hundred farmers want to get together to fight smaller groups of their neighbors? Because they can then take over their neighbors' land and have more food for themselves. If they choose to kill the neighbors, they can also take the neighbors' women as their wives. Or if they let the neighbors live, they can turn them into slaves to do some of the menial tasks that proliferated in complex agricultural societies.[18]

In fact, while the economic superiority of large groups helps explain their persistence, the immediate factor that led to their creation was virtually always military force.[19] Early farmers didn't just say, "Hey, let's get together so we can have more efficient division of labor and better public works projects!" Either they merged under the threat of military annihilation, or they were conquered and absorbed by another military power. History is full of examples of wars of conquest that created larger and larger organized groups: the Roman Empire, the empire of Alexander the Great, the Zulus in Africa, the Aztecs and Incas in America, and on and on.[20]

Why Were the Large Organizations Centralized?

There remains one puzzle: Why were these bigger organizations centralized? Why, for instance, didn't the large farming communities continue to use a decentralized, egalitarian structure? Why didn't they just organize into 100-person or even 10,000-person farming bands, with power and decision-making authority widely diffused among the members? Why did they turn to chiefs and headmen and, eventually, kings and emperors?

The short answer to this question, again, is communication costs. It was simply too expensive to have highly decentralized decision making in such large groups. When the only means of communication is face-to-face conversation, egalitarian decision making among a large number of people usually just takes too long. If decisions are made by consensus, the process rapidly becomes more unwieldy as the size of a group grows larger than one or two dozen people (as I saw with the antinuclear protesters in the preface). And, in contrast to the nomadic hunter-gatherer bands, in which dissenters to a group decision could easily move to another group, it would have been very difficult for dissenting farmers to leave their farms behind and try to find other farms elsewhere.

Even if the early farmers had considered the process of democratic voting (which may well not have even occurred to them), they still would have needed to spend large amounts of time educating each other about all the facts needed to make good decisions. Whether our ancestors liked it or not, their societies were just much more efficient when somebody was in charge and could gather information, make decisions, and tell everyone else what to do.

This choice to use centralized, hierarchical structures was not without its costs, however. For one thing, the leaders usually kept for themselves some—maybe even a lot—of the economic value created by the group. Some tribal chiefs in Hawaii, for instance, had cloaks fashioned of tens of thousands of brightly colored feathers. These cloaks were the result of the work of many, many generations of artisans.[21] It would be hard to argue that this incredibly ostentatious clothing for the chief—or, for that matter, the huge pyramids erected by the Egyptians to entomb their pharaohs—provided any significant public value for the other members of the tribe. But chiefs and kings were routinely able to get away with similar diversions of public resources for their own use. Evolutionary biologist Jared Diamond goes so far as to call all centralized governments "kleptocracies."[22]

Another—more intangible—cost of centralized organizations was the loss of individual autonomy. The move from hunting and gathering bands to hierarchical agricultural societies required all people, except perhaps the leaders, to sacrifice a portion of their freedom—in some cases, almost all of it.[23]

The Choice

This, then, was the profound organizational choice our ancestors made: to give up the freedom they had enjoyed as hunters and gatherers in order to obtain all the economic and military benefits offered by large, centralized hierarchies. They almost certainly did not think consciously about the choice in anything like the explicit terms we can use today. For many people, in fact, the choice was not even voluntary. They were simply defeated in battle and forced to live under someone else's rule. But time after time, in place after place, our ancestors collectively chose to move to a larger, centralized organization, rather than maintain their freedom and remain isolated. Our ancient ancestors first made this choice when they left the hunting life behind to become farmers. But they kept making the same choice time and again throughout thousands of years of history.

From Kingdoms to Democracies:
Printing, Citizens, and a Return to Decentralization

Sometime around 500 B.C., the Greeks developed a radical idea: that the people of a country were not the subjects of a king from whom power descended, but instead were the republic's citizens, from whom power ascended.[24] We now call this idea *democracy*. As shown in figure 2-1, every citizen in a democracy can (at least potentially) participate in making key decisions and communicate with everyone else. Democracy was possible in ancient Athens, even with its rudimentary communications system, because most Athenian citizens were literate (good!), but also because 60 percent to 80 percent of the population weren't citizens at all but rather slaves (bad!). The work of the slaves allowed the citizens enough leisure to participate in government.[25]

It wasn't until the late 1700s, however, that this radical idea began to take root in a widespread way. With the American and then the French revolutions, the world changed suddenly and fundamentally as people embarked upon a great new direction in societal organization. In the course of a few decades, the democratic notions of Athens were combined with a host of other new inventions: limitations on governmental power, representative assemblies, written constitutions, separation of powers, federalism, popularly approved laws, equal treatment under the law, freedom of speech, and freedom of the press, to name just a few.[26] Today, only about two hundred years later, governments all over the world have adopted these ideas. Although not all countries have become democracies, democratic principles now define many people's idea of a modern state.[27]

In just the last couple of hundred years, therefore, the great historical tide of centralization was reversed. Our ancestors chose to reclaim some of the freedom they had been systematically abandoning ever since they began moving to farms almost 12,000 years ago.

Why did such a prolonged historical trend suddenly change course? The new nations were not becoming significantly smaller, so people did not have to give up any of the economic or military benefits they received from larger organizations. But, for some reason, people believed they could now receive these benefits without giving up as much of their freedom. What could have caused this shift at this particular time?

As usual in human affairs, there were many factors. But one stands out as particularly important: our old friend, communication costs. In about 1450, Gutenberg developed the first movable-type printing press. This new technology, together with the rapidly expanding literacy it encouraged, dramatically decreased the costs of communicating in large groups. For the first time in history, it was economically possible for huge numbers of people, spread out over vast distances, to receive essentially the same message in relatively short amounts of time.

This much more intense communication—not just top-down, but also bottom-up and sideways—was necessary for large-scale democracies to work. The democratic ideal of government "of the people, by the people, and for the people" has little hope of success unless "the people" can be well enough informed to participate sensibly in the political process. And unless the people can make their desires known, they have little hope of influencing political outcomes.

Of course, the newly feasible democracies also gave people more of something that most humans want: freedom. More people could make more of their own choices about how they wanted to live their lives. But democracies also had another advantage: They were, in general, more flexible than the kingdoms they replaced. In democracies, lots of people can try lots of different things. They can express many points of view about problems and solutions. Moreover, any small group would have difficulty preventing changes that most people think are good. As Philip Slater and Warren Bennis argued in a prophetic 1964 article, "Democracy Is Inevitable," democracies are simply more efficient at surviving in conditions of chronic change.[28]

In fact, from a historical perspective, the democratic phase of our human political development has probably not even begun to run its course. Even in countries in which the citizens democratically elect representatives to make their political decisions, most of the rest of modern government is still relatively centralized. One sign of what may be in store for us is Western politicians' growing reliance on increasingly sophisticated opinion polling to influence "small" decisions between elections. Whether you think this is a good development or not, it is certainly happening more frequently. And it is clearly an example of decentralizing even more decision making to the citizens of a democracy.

The Choice

The answer, then, to the question of why our ancestors could suddenly change course and choose decentralization is this: New technologies like the printing press reduced communication costs enough that people were able to have two things they wanted without having to choose between them. They could retain the economic and military benefits of large organizations while also regaining some of the freedom and flexibility they had given up long ago. As we will see, the same possibility is now opening up for us in business.

CHAPTER THREE

The Amazing Pattern in Business

NIKE, the athletic apparel manufacturer, outsources all its manufacturing to other companies. Hewlett-Packard surveys its own employees to see whether they think it should merge with Compaq. British Petroleum divides itself into ninety business units, each with an average of fewer than six hundred employees. One of the best computer operating systems in the world is developed not by a company but by a loose network of thousands of volunteers.[1]

What's going on here?

Remarkably, the same pattern of organizational change that occurred in society is also unfolding—though much more rapidly—in business. As figure 3-1 indicates, the first and second stages of the pattern are already largely complete, as large, centralized corporate hierarchies have come to replace small, more informally organized businesses over the last two hundred years. But the last stage—from corporate hierarchies to more decentralized business networks—is only now beginning.

From Small Businesses to Corporate Hierarchies

Up until about 1800, most businesses in the world were small family affairs. In 1790, for instance, 90 percent of the U.S. labor force lived and worked on farms. Family farmers not only produced crops for market, but also raised much of their own food and made their own furniture, soap, candles, and clothing.[2] Most of the commercial manufacturing in the United States was done by artisans—weavers, tanners, blacksmiths, wagon makers—who lived above or near their shops.[3]

FIGURE 3-1

*The major changes in how businesses were organized throughout history
echo the changes in how societies were organized.*

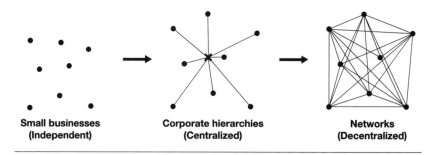

Small businesses	Corporate hierarchies	Networks
(Independent)	(Centralized)	(Decentralized)

Even in cities, family businesses and small partnerships dominated commerce. Alfred Chandler describes the operation of a small merchant's office in New York in the early 1800s: "Inside the counting house—the term first used by the Italians for a merchant's office—a business was carried on in much the same manner as it had been in fourteenth century Venice or Florence. The staff included only a handful of male clerks. There were two or three copiers, a bookkeeper, a cash keeper, and a confidential clerk who handled the business when the partners were not in the office. The organization and coordination of work in such an office could easily be arranged in a personal daily conversation."[4]

Although such early businesses differed in many ways from ancient hunter-gatherer tribes, their organizational structures had interesting similarities. Both were small, local groups whose members communicated through face-to-face conversations, enjoyed a fair amount of personal freedom, and rarely interacted with the members of other groups. Even though farming was associated with increased centralization in the evolution of society, from a business point of view, farmers continued to have a great deal of freedom. With long-distance communication still very costly, farmers and other people who ran small businesses had no choice but to make their own decisions based mostly on the information they could gather locally.

The Beginnings of Corporate Hierarchies

In the centuries before 1800, a few nongovernmental organizations developed large, multilevel, centralized hierarchies. The Phoenician traders of the eighth century B.C., the Catholic Church, and the Hudson Bay Company are three examples.[5] But it was not until the 1800s that this hierarchical form of organization began to become common in business.

The railroad industry was one of the first to embrace centralization. By the 1870s, explains Chandler, the large railroads in Europe and the United States had managerial hierarchies that would look quite familiar to most modern business people: "Middle and top managers supervised, coordinated, and evaluated the work of lower level managers who were directly responsible for the day-to-day operations. . . . [T]op management included the president, . . . the treasurer . . . and a general manager who supervised the work of two or three general superintendents. By then middle management included the general superintendents, their assistants, and the heads of machinery, . . . maintenance, . . . freight, passenger, and purchasing."[6]

This remarkable new form of corporate organization expanded rapidly, coming to dominate businesses all over the world in the 1900s. Indeed, the ability to establish such an organization soon came to be viewed as one of the hallmarks of business success. Even today, many small, decentralized organizations hope that someday they'll become big, centralized ones. And for good reason: Big companies have delivered amazing material benefits and have largely shaped the world in which we live and work today.

What Caused the Rise of Corporate Hierarchies?

As usual, many factors contributed to the rise of large, centralized organizations. The two most important, though, are the same ones that drove the shift to centralized governments: the declining costs of communication and the benefits of bigness.

The benefits of bigness, in this case, often came through the economies of scale enabled by the new technologies of mass production. As Chandler puts it, "a single set of workers using a single set of facilities [could] handle a much greater number of transactions within a specific period than the same number of workers could if they had been scattered in many separate small facilities."[7] The epitome of the new way of organizing work was the moving assembly line. Two years after Henry Ford and his colleagues introduced the automotive assembly line in 1913, the amount of time it took workers to make a model T had dropped from 12 hours and 8 minutes, to 1 hour and 33 minutes.[8]

The economic benefits of bigness would not have been possible, however, without a decrease in communication costs. To sell their mass-produced products, firms like Ford's needed much larger markets, which in turn required much tighter coordination of business activities. This coordination would not have been possible without the new communication and transportation technologies of the railroad, the telegraph, and, eventually, the telephone.

These new technologies enabled businesses to bring large amounts of information from far-flung regions to a central headquarters. There, a company's top managers could take a broader perspective—national or even global—and make better decisions than independent, local businesspeople could. By reducing the costs and delays in sending messages (and moving products) over long distances, these new technologies both increased the size of markets and enabled the much richer communication needed to coordinate large-scale operations. In general, the companies that figured out how to do things in these new ways either eliminated their competitors or forced them to change, too.

The Choice

Just as our ancient ancestors chose to give up some of their freedom to get the benefits of bigness in their political lives, many of our own grandparents made a similar choice in their business lives. Time after time, they gave up the freedom and informality of family farms and other small businesses for the unprecedented prosperity—and the increased control—of the assembly line and the corporate office. The new communication technologies of the nineteenth and twentieth centuries made this choice possible for them, and now it's hard for us to imagine them having made any other choice.

From Corporate Hierarchies to Networks

The main story about the organization of business in the twentieth century was centralization, and a glance at today's headlines about huge acquisitions and megamergers reveals that this story is still continuing in some parts of the economy. AOL buys Time Warner. Citibank and Travelers merge to become Citigroup. Price Waterhouse merges with Coopers & Lybrand to become PricewaterhouseCoopers (PwC), and then IBM buys the consulting arm of PwC. A single company, Wal-Mart, has more than a 30 percent share of the market for general merchandise retailing.

But beneath the headlines, we find a more complex story. Some tantalizing signs of a new and very different trend are appearing. In a study that my colleagues and I published in the mid-1990s, we found evidence that the average size of firms in many U.S. industries was actually declining.[9] One way companies shrink is through increased outsourcing. When big companies offload work to contractors, they may end up controlling ever-larger flows of cash, but they exert less and less direct control over actual business activity. They buy more of the things they need from outsiders rather than making these items themselves. Some companies, like Nike and Cisco Systems, have handed over almost all their production to subcontractors. Even routine tasks are often being carried out not by employees but by temporary workers. Indeed, the largest private employer in the United States today is not General Motors or IBM or even Wal-Mart. It's the temporary-employment agency Manpower Incorporated, which in 2002 "employed" 2 million people.[10]

Big companies are, you might say, growing hollow.

There's another, related trend: Informal, ever-shifting alliances of people and firms—variously called virtual corporations, networked organizations, business webs, and corporate *keiretsu*—are performing more and more of the work that used to be done inside large organizations.[11] In the personal computer industry, for example, Intel and Microsoft form the nucleus of a complex ecology of computer hardware makers, software developers, and professional services firms. Just thirty years ago, the functions performed by this complex web of companies would have been carried out entirely within the walls of IBM.

Even within large corporations, highly centralized command-and-control management is becoming less common. Decisions are being pushed lower down through the ranks.[12] In a detailed study of three hundred large U.S. firms, Raghuram Rajan and Julie Wulf found substantial evidence that hierarchies were flattening and lower-level managers were being treated more like owners.[13] Between 1984 and 1999, the number of positions reporting directly to the CEO in these firms rose significantly, the number of levels between division heads and the CEO decreased, and more and more employees received long-term pay incentives like stock and stock options.

In many cases, workers are being rewarded not for efficiently carrying out orders but for figuring out what needs to be done and then doing it. Some large industrial companies like Asea Brown Boveri and British Petroleum have even broken themselves up into scores of independent units that conduct business with one another almost as if they were separate companies.

Such decentralization initiatives appear to be paying off. In one intriguing survey, my MIT colleagues Erik Brynjolfsson and Lorin Hitt found that firms that had decentralized decision making—for example, by establishing self-managing teams or allowing individuals greater discretion in doing work—were significantly more likely to have higher market valuations than comparable firms that made decisions in more traditional ways.[14]

What is behind this new trend? No one knows for sure. Certainly, there are many contributing factors: increasing globalization, increasing education and affluence, and many others. In fact, to many people, the signs of decentralization are just isolated exceptions in a world of ever-increasing centralization.

But before you slip comfortably into that easy assumption, it's worth thinking back to how cheaper communication led to the breakup of highly centralized forms of government. A similar force appears to be at work in business today.

Decreased Communication Costs Make Decentralization Possible

We've already seen how the printing press helped unleash the great democratic ferment of the late 1700s. But even though books and newspapers transformed political communication, they were rarely used for business communication. With the exception of advertising, most business communication in the 1800s and early 1900s still occurred through one-to-one media: face-to-face conversations, letters, memos, telegrams, and telephone calls.[15] Arguably, businesses didn't truly begin to make significant use of one-to-many communication vehicles until after the Xerox machine became popular in the 1960s.

The 1990s have seen an explosion in one-to-many and many-to-many media for business communication: e-mail, conference calls, the Web, and so forth. Today, anyone with access to the Internet can find—almost immediately and often at no cost—a greater wealth of information on many subjects than was available to even the most elite decision makers at the tops of huge organizations like IBM, General Motors, and the U.S. government only a few decades ago.

Now, why should this matter? In a centralized hierarchy, relatively little communication is required, because, in general, information only

---

Consider the cost of sending one page of text to 100 people scattered across the United States. As table 3-1 shows, in the 1840s (before railroads) mailing such a letter would have cost about $100, and it would have taken about eleven days to reach the recipients. With railroads, the cost would have fallen to $85 and the delay to about two and a half days. With the telegraph, the cost increased to about $750 but the delay was decreased to a few hours. With modern e-mail systems, the cost of sending one message to 100 people is essentially $0 and delivery is almost instantaneous.[16]

TABLE 3-1

Delay and Cost for Transmitting One Page of Text via Different Media

Medium	DELAY IN HOURS		COST	
	1 Destination	100 Destinations	1 Destination	100 Destinations
Pre-railroad Mail, 1840s	252.000	260.3	$0.25	$107.17
Railroad, 1850s	48.000	56.3	$0.03	$85.17
Telegraph, 1850s	0.083	8.3	$7.50	$750.00
E-mail, 2000s	~0	~0	~0	~0

needs to be communicated once to a single place—the top of the hierarchy. In a decentralized system, however, many more people make decisions, and they all need information. Today's new communication technologies make an efficient, decentralized system possible for the first time. Suddenly, it's cheap and easy for lots of people in an organization to get lots of information quickly and without distortion.

The same basic reasoning applies to the outsourcing of work.[17] To hand off an activity to another company, you have to do a number of things: find potential suppliers, compare them and make selections, place orders, make payments, coordinate deliveries, and adjust to any changes along the way. When you only have traditional media, like face-to-face meetings and letters, carrying out all those tasks takes a lot of time and money. It's often easier just to use an internal supplier. But when all the necessary communication becomes cheap and convenient, outsourcing becomes more common. Our research backs up this point. We've found that when an industry makes greater use of information technology, the average size of companies in that industry tends to decrease after a lag of about two years.[18]

Other Factors Make Decentralization Desirable

Technology makes many changes possible, but only those that fulfill people's needs and desires actually happen. Decentralized organizations are attractive because they give more people more freedom. The result is both economic and noneconomic benefits.

Economic Benefits: Motivation, Creativity, and Flexibility   When people make their own decisions about how to do their work and allocate their time, they often put more energy, effort, and creativity into their jobs.[19] Studies of R&D projects, for instance, have found that when the members of project teams feel more freedom and control over their work, they become more innovative.[20] That sense of autonomy is probably part of entrepreneurial motivation, too: Not only do you keep the economic rewards of your own work, but you also can make your own decisions and feel like an owner.

When people feel tightly controlled, by contrast, they are often less motivated and less creative. Albert Einstein put it well when he remembered the militaristic school he attended as a child: "This coercion had such a deterring effect upon me that, after I had passed the final examination, I found the consideration of any scientific problems distasteful for an entire year."[21]

In addition to strengthening motivation, decentralized systems can accommodate much more flexibility. Many minds can be working on the same problem at once. Lots of people can be trying lots of approaches, and the ones that work best can be adopted elsewhere. And decisions, instead of being handed down from some distant headquarters, can be tailored to immediate local conditions. Locally based decision making had advantages in the past: A small-town store owner, for instance, could give credit and recommend products based on a deep knowledge of each of his or her customers. And localized decisions can pay off today as well: An autonomous salesperson can make on-the-spot pricing decisions based on the look in the customer's eyes— together with, perhaps, electronically supplied information on manufacturing costs.

Noneconomic Benefits: Freedom and Individualization   Decentralization offers personal as well as economic satisfaction. Many people simply like having the freedom to make their own choices.[22] When they have more freedom, their work becomes more interesting and enjoyable, and they're better able to juggle the various demands that life places on them. If, for example, they have control over when and how they work, they can more easily manage other important commitments like caring for their children or spending time with their aging parents.

The Amazing Pattern

Here, then, is the basic three-stage pattern that we've seen in both societies and business organizations: In stage one, people operate in small, unconnected groups. In stage two, much larger groups are formed and decision making becomes centralized. In the third stage, the large groups remain, but decision making becomes more decentralized.

This pattern is an excellent example of the kind of phenomena that coordination theory analyzes. Through a detailed study of this particular pattern, my colleagues and I have gained a much more precise understanding of when and how organizational forms change (see the appendix for a summary of our research). One of our findings supports a conclusion made by many other researchers: that greater use of information technology can lead to either centralization or decentralization, depending on the situation.[23] Our model shows, for example, how information technology can enable more centralization when economies of scale are important and more decentralization when motivation and flexibility are important.

But our model goes further than most previous work. It reveals that the benefits of centralization are often the benefits of bigness, not benefits of centralization itself. And, in many cases, when communication gets cheap enough, you can afford to decentralize in a way that gives you both the benefits of bigness, like scale economies, and the benefits of smallness, like motivation and flexibility.[24]

When the benefits of smallness are important (but not as important as the benefits of bigness), our model predicts that a two-step process should occur. First, decreasing communication costs should lead to increasing centralization, until the benefits of bigness have been captured. Then, eventually, further decreases in communication costs should lead to increasing decentralization.[25] This pattern of initial increase and then subsequent decrease in centralization is exactly what appears to be happening in many parts of business. Centralization has been increasing until fairly recently, but is now beginning to decrease in many places. We can expect to see more of this decentralization wherever (a) communication costs are falling and (b) motivation, creativity, flexibility, and the other benefits of smallness produce business gains.

As it turns out, those two criteria hold true across huge swaths of today's economy. Information technology is relentlessly pushing down communication costs, enabling companies to decentralize without sacrificing scale economies. And the increasing importance of knowledge work makes motivation, creativity, and flexibility more important than ever.

Does this mean that everything will become decentralized? Of course not. Centralized structures will continue to make sense where the benefits of smallness are insignificant relative to the benefits of bigness, or where there's just no way to get enough of the benefits of bigness in a decentralized system.

Have we even proven, beyond a shadow of a doubt, that the amazing pattern is actually happening in business? No. As with any scientific theory, there could be some other explanation for all the phenomena we've explored in this chapter.[26] But the logic of our model, combined with the pervasiveness of the pattern in history, certainly provides compelling evidence that we're in the midst of a fundamental and predictable change—one that may be as important to business as the shift to democracy has been to government. And even if it turns out that this shift will only affect a relatively small part of the economy, it will still be critical for you to know whether you are in that part. And if you are, you need to know how you can take advantage of the changes.

The Choice

Decentralized business organizations represent a new world of work, with new rules and new demands. Just as the democratic political assumptions we take for granted today would have seemed almost incomprehensible to the loyal subjects of King Carlos IV of Spain, the basic assumptions of the decentralized world seem strange to most of us today. As we make the choices that will define this world, we will need new examples, new principles, and new practices. We will need to know how to imagine new possibilities, how to artfully combine the benefits of centralization with those of decentralization, and how to think differently about management.

Meeting those challenges is the focus of the rest of this book.

II

How Many People Can Fit at the Center of an Organization?

CHAPTER FOUR

Loosening the Hierarchy

WHEN GOOGLE, the Web search firm, starts a major project, it doesn't create a huge new organization with lots of management layers. Instead, it sets up a few small, autonomous engineering teams—often of only about three members each—and sets them loose, giving them wide latitude in how they do their work.[1]

When the teams need to exchange information, they often don't need to involve managers at all. Instead, they communicate directly, either face-to-face or electronically. In early 2003, Google started using a system to help teams keep Web logs, or *blogs,* that chronicle their day-to-day activities, discoveries, and problems. Within weeks, the use of these online diaries had exploded. By reading the blogs, the different teams could keep track of one another's work and find issues that needed further discussion—with less need for top-down control by centralized managers.

This simple example illustrates one important way that big organizations can decentralize decision making: loose hierarchies. This chapter will describe loose hierarchies in detail. Chapters 5, 6, and 7 will then consider the two other main ways of decentralizing decisions: democracies and markets.

A Loose Hierarchy for Software Development

One of the best-known examples of a loose hierarchy is the group of people who developed the Linux computer operating system for personal computers. The group originated in 1991, when twenty-one-year-old Linus Torvalds made available on the Internet a rudimentary kernel of an operating system he had written. He encouraged other people to use and modify it for free, and eventually thousands of volunteer programmers all over the world were fixing bugs, adding features, and writing documentation. Today, Linux has become one of the best operating systems available, and many people consider it the single most serious challenger to Microsoft Windows for dominance in the world of operating systems.

The Linux story is a well-known example of so-called open-source software—software available for free to anyone who wants to use or modify it. A less well known aspect of the Linux story is its new, highly decentralized way of organizing knowledge work.

Loose hierarchies like Linux's share three salient characteristics. First, they have dense communication. No matter how far-flung, the members need to stay in close touch with one another. A huge project like Linux simply couldn't have existed without the cheap, worldwide communication provided by the Internet.

Second, the Linux group has a relative lack of centralized control. Even though the thousands of people working on Linux produced a very good and very complex product, they didn't do it in anything like the centralized, hierarchical way that Microsoft or IBM develops complex software products. The Linux group does have a hierarchy, but most decisions are delegated to a very low level in the organization. In fact, only two types of decisions are centralized: (1) Torvalds himself established the overarching goal, that is, to implement a version of the UNIX operating system for PCs, and (2) Torvalds and a few of his trusted lieutenants decide which of the many changes people suggest will be included in new releases of the system. All the other decisions are delegated to the volunteer programmers, each of whom chooses which tasks to do, when to do them, how to do them, and whom (if anyone) to work with.

Third, the members of loose hierarchies have freedom to participate. They can join or drop out of the effort whenever they feel like it. For a loose hierarchy to work, therefore, a project must appeal to the values—whatever they are—of the people required to complete it. It's possible, as we'll see in chapter 6, to use traditional economic incentives to motivate people in loose hierarchies. But most people who contribute to Linux are pure volunteers. They don't do it for the money; they do it because it satisfies their other human values.

Many programmers cherish, for example, the recognition and status of having their contributions included in the Linux system. There's even a word for this in the technical community: *egoboo*. Short for "ego boost," egoboo is the satisfaction you get from being praised for a job well done.[2] Of course, egoboo has always motivated people in their work, but many centralized hierarchies vastly underestimate its power.

By delegating decision making and engaging people's values, loose hierarchies can take advantage of a much greater amount of creativity and energy from a much larger pool of people than would ever be possible in most traditional companies. And, as we'll see next, this decentralized approach is not limited to software. It can be used for many other kinds of intellectual products as well.

An Even Looser Hierarchy for Creating an Encyclopedia

In January 2001, Larry Sanger and Jimmy Wales decided to develop a new encyclopedia on the Web.[3] But they didn't hire layers of editors and subeditors for the various subject areas. Nor did they contract with experts to write, illustrate, and review all the articles. They didn't even plan to revise and polish each entry before publishing it.

Instead, inspired by open-source software, they created an "open-content" encyclopedia. First, they set up a basic Web site for the encyclopedia and called it Wikipedia (www.wikipedia.org). *Wiki,* the Hawaiian term for "quick," refers to the ease with which people can add and edit entries using the special collaboration software the site used.[4] Then, Sanger and Wales and a few of their friends started writing and posting articles, making them freely available to anyone on the Web. And here's the really unusual thing: the group let anyone, at any time, revise the existing articles or add new articles of their own.

No centralized quality control. No systematic peer reviewing. No editorial approvals. Other than Sanger, who was paid by Wales's Internet portal company as an informal chief organizer for the first two years of the project, everyone else was a volunteer.

The response was phenomenal. In the first month, Wikipedia had 1,000 articles. After the first year, it had 20,000; after the second, it had 100,000. By mid-2003, more than seven hundred people had listed themselves as contributors, more than ten thousand had registered as users, and an unknown number of others had contributed anonymously.

"OK," you may be thinking, "I can believe that some people might do this for fun, but how good are the articles?" The answer is: pretty darn good. While it doesn't yet rival, say, the *Encyclopedia Britannica* in quantity or quality, Wikipedia already has a substantial store of well-written, accurate content. The site lists as examples of especially well written entries, articles on alchemy, DNA, menstrual cycle, prisoner's dilemma, World War I, poker, and Humphrey Bogart.

Several factors appear to contribute to the relatively high quality. First, highly educated, skilled writers have been attracted by the idea of collectively creating a global encyclopedia that is free to everyone. As a newspaper columnist in Nashua, New Hampshire, wrote, "I . . . stumbled across Wikipedia, and now I'm hooked. I've become an information-is-free addict, and I'll tell you more as soon as I finish updating the Wikipedia entry on Holman Stadium [Nashua's baseball park]."[5]

Second, frequent contributors make a point of reviewing new and updated pages for everything from spelling mistakes to factual errors. In some cases, they fix errors immediately. In others, they add the entry to an online list entitled "Pages needing attention." Many Wikipedians subscribe to a fundamental belief underpinning open-source software: Given enough eyeballs, all errors are shallow.

Third, one of the site's policies is that all articles must be written from a neutral point of view. For controversial topics, the contributors try to describe the alternative perspectives fairly, rather than advocating any one of them. This policy is only enforced by the voluntary actions of people who write and edit the pages, but it seems to be widely followed and to contribute to the feeling of a constructive, collaborative community.

Finally, on rare occasions, vandals have made malicious changes to pages. In these cases, the culprit's access to the site has been curtailed by a volunteer administrator.

What is the role of the managers of this system? Here's how the Wikipedia article, "Wikipedia," answers that question:

> There is no editor-in-chief per se. The two people who founded Wikipedia, Jimmy Wales (CEO of the small Internet company Bomis, Inc.) and Larry Sanger [a recent philosophy Ph.D.], like to think of themselves as participants who are charged with see-

ing to it that the project does not stray from the path on which it is already travelling.

For the first years (and a few months) of Wikipedia's existence, Larry was a paid employee. His job was to oversee Wikipedia (and Nupedia); with the advice of everyone, it was his responsibility to make final, fair decisions on issues where community consensus could not be reached. Funding ran out for his position, leading to his resignation, but he still contributes occasionally.

Jimmy and Wikipedians as a whole have taken over some of Larry's former responsibilities.[6]

Wikipedia is about as extreme a form of loose hierarchy as can be imagined. Wales and Sanger were influential in setting an original direction and some guiding policies. But thereafter, their managerial roles diminished. Now, with the project's foundations in place, the community operates effectively, with very little management intervention.

It is too soon to tell whether this project will succeed in its goal of creating the "largest encyclopedia in history."[7] But its success so far shows that amazingly loose hierarchies can create impressively large and complex results.

The success of Wikipedia also shows that noneconomic motivations—in the right circumstances—can cause people to do things that you might have thought would require serious financial investments. Surprisingly, unlike with Linux, the desire for personal recognition doesn't even appear to be a primary motivator for most contributors to Wikipedia. Since all articles are unsigned and most are edited by a number of people, individual authors receive no public credit. For most people, the main attraction is probably the intellectually addictive pleasure of the task itself, the remarkable freedom everyone has to improve the product, and the satisfaction of working together toward a grand vision.

Loose Hierarchies in Consulting Firms and Research Universities

Linux and Wikipedia are hierarchies so open that many people might not even call them organizations at all. But extensive delegation occurs in much more conventional organizations as well. In many large management consulting firms, for example, most operational decisions are delegated to the individual partners and other consultants who manage projects. For the most part, partners and senior consultants decide for themselves what kinds of projects to do, which clients to pursue, and how to accomplish their assignments. The top managers of these firms don't focus on managing the actual consulting work, but rather on evaluating and rewarding the people who do perform it. Many firms devote extensive resources to this process. McKinsey, for instance, gives enormous attention to recruiting and promotion decisions, often soliciting input on candidates for promotion to partner from dozens of other people in the firm.

By delegating so much control to "line" consultants, consulting firms obtain many of the benefits of decentralized organizations. Individual consultants have a great deal of autonomy and, as a result, are often highly motivated and creative. Also, because so many consultants are constantly trying to sell projects to clients, the whole organization is extremely sensitive to changes in what clients want. The firm can therefore usually adapt quickly to market shifts.

In a similar vein, most research universities give individual professors a great deal of freedom. For example, one of the things I liked best about MIT when I first arrived was that I didn't really have a boss. Sure, there was a group head and an area head and a dean, all of whom were somehow above me in the management structure, but none of them really acted as a boss. Senior faculty members played a big role in mentoring me and would eventually decide whether I was promoted and tenured, but no one told me what to do in the way a typical boss would. Like the other faculty members in my department, I was a kind of independent entrepreneur, ultimately deciding for myself what to do and how to do it. In a sense, each of us was at the center of our own organization, doing our own things.

Many people, of course, think of universities as sloppy, poorly managed organizations. But in spite of its loose hierarchical structure, MIT is still extremely effective at doing cutting-edge research and delivering quality education. Perhaps MIT is so successful at this kind of knowledge work *because* it has such a loose hierarchical structure. If MIT were managed in a tighter, more hierarchical way, it might never attract the kind of creative people it needs to be successful. And, perhaps, if MIT's administrators tried to control the research and teaching of their faculty members more closely, the quality of the work would go down, not up.

Good research universities adapt well to changing research directions in different fields. That's not because the deans and department chairs necessarily have a good sense of what kind of research should be done at any given moment. It's because the organization lets individual professors follow their noses to the best problems, and then it rewards the people who are successful.

Extreme Delegation in AES

"Well," you may now be thinking, "I can see how this kind of thing could work in weird organizations like universities and consulting firms and software development groups, but it would never work in a real company." If you think that, though, you're wrong. While loose hierarchies are far from common in large industrial companies, some companies have adopted these structures—and they're working.

Perhaps the most extreme example is AES Corporation. Founded in 1981 by Chairman Roger Sant and now retired CEO Dennis Bakke, the company has become one of the largest suppliers of electric power in the world. In 2002, it had revenues of $8.6 billion and about 36,000 employees in twenty-eight countries.[8]

What's most unusual about AES is its management philosophy. The two founders emphasize four guiding principles they want AES to embody: fairness, integrity, social responsibility, and fun. Now, many companies *talk* about noneconomic values like these, but AES appears to have gone much further than most in actually building its business around them.

In particular, it puts great emphasis on the last principle—fun. According to Bakke, "We never set out to be the most efficient or most powerful or richest company in the world—only the most fun."[9] The founders believe that one of the best ways for people to have fun is to have responsibility for things that truly matter in the world. When you're responsible for something, you usually put your heart, mind, and soul into it in a way that you never would if you were just following orders.

Consequently, AES has been built on the idea that every employee should be a businessperson—a well-rounded generalist, a mini-CEO—responsible for important decisions in the company. The biggest economic decision the company has ever made was buying Drax, a power station in England, in late 1999. But, says Bakke, this decision "was not made by me. It was not made by the board. It was not made by the fourteen group managers. It was made by a person who had been with this company not quite two years and I had not even met him."[10] The young man who made the decision received advice—mostly by e-mail—from all kinds of people throughout the company. But in the end, the final decision about whether to make the purchase and how much to offer was his.

In another example, a group of maintenance workers at a plant in Connecticut were put in charge of investing a $12 million cash reserve in the short-term money market. They hired a finance teacher and started talking to brokers on Wall Street. By the third month, the group had beat the returns of the people who were investing money for the company's treasury at the home office. Says Bakke: "Did letting the maintenance crew invest that money make a huge difference in our bottom line, for better or for worse? Probably not. But those people will be changed forever. They have become better businesspeople. And there is no other way to do that than by doing."[11] AES has dozens of stories like this one: very young or inexperienced people acquiring plants or making other decisions involving many millions of dollars, with lots of advice but with no need for approval from anyone else.

AES's philosophy is to treat everyone as responsible, accountable adults, not as children who have to be constantly supervised and instructed. In doing this, AES sees itself as explicitly undoing some of the assumptions about people that became common in the industrial revolution. Back then, according to Bakke and AES board member Bob Waterman, organizations were designed as if people coming off the farms to work in factories couldn't be trusted, weren't very good at making decisions, had to be trained, and wouldn't work unless you told them what to do.[12] Whether these assumptions were ever true is certainly debatable, but many of today's corporations are still designed as if they were. AES, on the other hand, assumes that people are unique—if fallible—adults, that they want and can handle responsibility, and that they are thoughtful, creative, and trustworthy.

To put its philosophy into practice, AES uses a combination of methods. First, the company is very careful about hiring. Many job candidates are referred to the company by current employees, and before anyone is hired, he or she goes through an extensive qualification process, with team interviews, multiple meetings, and intensive peer review. Interviewers pay a great deal of attention to questions of cultural fit, rarely focusing on technical ability until fairly late in the process. When AES acquires other companies, which it does regularly, it devotes a great deal of effort to teaching the acquired companies' employees the AES values. Employees who don't fit well with the value system usually choose to leave—in some cases taking loans from AES to help them start new businesses.[13]

The AES philosophy wouldn't work without extensive communication. Even though no one has to get approvals or sign-offs or reach consensus before making a decision, there is one rule: The person has to get advice. And the people making the decision are the ones who decide where to go for the advice. Usually, the bigger the decision, the more advice they get and the "higher" in the company they go to get it.

Although AES was founded before e-mail became prevalent, this electronic medium has allowed the AES communication-intensive decision-making process to work on a much larger scale than before. According to Bakke, "e-mail has blossomed into a major part of how the company works."[14] Bakke himself says that, when he was CEO, he would usually receive thirty to fifty requests for advice every day.

The free-flowing communication means that all kinds of financial and market information, even the details of potential acquisitions, are shared widely throughout the company. Information that, in many companies, would only be available to the board of directors and very senior executives bounces around in e-mails and conversations at all levels of AES. The U.S. Securities and Exchange Commission restricts the stock trading that people with this kind of inside information can make. In most companies, this restriction applies only to directors and a few senior executives. But because of the free flow of sensitive information in AES, every one of its employees is considered an insider for this purpose.

Is this free-flowing communication a good idea? Bakke summarizes the risks and rewards: "Some people are worried about how public we are with our information; they're concerned it's going to get leaked to competitors. But we think that's a risk worth taking because, otherwise, how would our people become businesspeople? You need information to make good decisions."[15]

What, then, is left for managers to do in AES? Bakke lists four key roles for bosses: (1) when asked, act as advisers to people throughout the company, (2) serve as chief guardians of the core principles of the organization, (3) set up the organizational structure, and (4) pick who will make a decision, in cases where that's not clear.[16]

Even though AES is experimenting with having teams and individuals set their own salaries, managers also still play a key role in determining pay and bonuses. Otherwise, all the key strategic, financial, and other decisions in the company are made by people close to the actual problems and opportunities, not by senior executives far away from the action. In one recent year, Bakke says that he made only two decisions: how many regional groups to have and who would lead them.[17]

Now, you may be wondering, is all this real? Is AES just telling a good story while acting how most companies have acted for years? As I listened to Bakke and others talk about the AES story, I came to believe that they had come up with something real—and extremely interesting.

The AES managers have given up less power than might at first appear. They say that lower-level people make lots of decisions, but these people have to obtain advice from many people (including managers). Moreover, the compensation and career prospects of lower-level employees are based heavily on evaluations by these same managers. So it would be unusual for people to make decisions that differed radically from what their senior managers recommended.

On the other hand, many traditional companies go out of their way to prevent low-level (or even middle- and upper-level) people from making decisions they aren't "supposed" to make. The AES philosophy does indeed appear to give many more people far greater power than do typical corporations. While it can't be definitively proven, you have to suspect that this freedom has something to do with the energy, excitement, decision-making speed, and amazingly rapid growth that AES has displayed over the two decades of its existence.

Would this approach work in other companies? Chairman Roger Sant puts it this way: "I would not recommend that other businesses adopt only our mechanics. They'd have to adopt some shared values first. . . .

But if companies adopt a set of shared principles, then the mechanics can be put in place." Bakke, however, worries that most executives aren't amenable to a dramatically less hierarchical organization: "I don't think it has happened in any other organizations because . . . people are not willing to give up their power, starting with the CEO and the board. Without them, it's futile to even try."[18]

This, then, is one of the fundamental choices that people holding power in successful businesses have to face: Are we willing to give up some of our control in order to create organizations that may work far better than before?

Lessons About Loose Hierarchies

All hierarchies, regardless of how much delegation goes on, have a common communication structure: Information is collected in a central point, where executives make decisions that govern their subordinates. When you agree to be part of such a system, you implicitly agree to abide by the decisions of your superiors. And if you do the things they want, they reward you.

Hierarchies offer some important benefits. They're good, for example, at coordinating large-scale systems with relatively little communication. Even in the loose Linux hierarchy, Linus Torvalds doesn't have to micromanage what people do on a daily basis. His central position nevertheless allows him to make sure that the software components he accepts for the final system are compatible with each other and with the overall goals of the project.

Hierarchies are also good, at least in principle, at resolving difficult conflicts of interest. When there is no higher authority, autonomous individuals (like feudal lords, partners in a consulting firm, or university professors) can often squabble forever without ever agreeing to do things that would, in the end, benefit them all. As a top manager in a centralized hierarchy, you can tell people what to do, and they'll usually comply with little discussion. The looser the hierarchy, however, the less frequently and the more delicately you need to wield such authority.

The strengths of hierarchies are balanced by weaknesses. First, managers can easily become overloaded, since many decisions have to

---

Hierarchies: Definition

Communication Structure

How Are Decisions Made?

Top-down authority (your decisions apply to your subordinates)

Scope of Decision Making

Once you agree to be part of the system, you must abide by the decisions of your superiors.

Incentives

Please your superiors (and they will reward you).

---

go up the management chain. In fact, sometimes we even gauge how important managers are by how long we have to wait for them to get back to us! Even in the Linux organization, if Torvalds or one of his key lieutenants becomes overloaded (or takes a long vacation), the whole system may slow down.

Second, since each person in a hierarchy works only on the tasks assigned to him or her, no one except the people at the very top may see the whole picture. AES tries to temper this problem by rotating people through many kinds of jobs and encouraging them to get many kinds of advice in making decisions. But at the end of the day, only the CEO and the board of directors truly own the problem of how the whole company works together.

In large hierarchies, managers don't even know all the individual strengths and weaknesses of the people who work for them. As a result, the managers may not assign the best people to each task. When low-level decision makers in AES seek advice, for example, they rely on a wide network of informal referrals to find people to ask—but they still may overlook the people who could actually be most helpful.

Hierarchies: Evaluation

Strengths

- Hierarchies can coordinate large-scale systems with relatively little communication.
- Strong hierarchies can resolve difficult conflicts of interest among individuals for the good of the group and can get compliance quickly (without a lot of discussion).

Weaknesses

- Each person works only on the parts of the problem assigned to him or her (which may not be the parts to which the person can contribute the most).
- If large amounts of information processing are needed, key nodes may be overloaded and become bottlenecks.
- At each level, one decision maker can veto any options he or she doesn't like. Often only one option is seriously explored.
- It is often hard to maintain a sense of autonomy in people.

Third, at each level in a hierarchy, a single decision maker can veto any options he or she doesn't like. This reduces the amount of communication needed (since no one else needs to consider the option), but it also makes hierarchies vulnerable to bad decisions at every level. Often, only one option is seriously explored, and if that is the wrong one, it may take a long time for the hierarchy to recover. If Torvalds, for example, makes a wrong decision about a key technical direction, a recovery from the mistake may be much more difficult than if many different alternatives had been explored along the way.

Finally, in hierarchies, you are always taking direction from people above you. For this reason, you may have a hard time maintaining a sense of autonomy and motivation. In traditional hierarchies, this lack of self-direction can be a very big problem. Many Dilbert cartoons capture perfectly the difficulty of maintaining any sense of motivation or creativity in your work when you are toiling away in your cubicle, a cog in the machinery of a senseless, authoritarian hierarchy.

The goal for any hierarchical organization is to balance the strengths and weaknesses of a hierarchy. Loose hierarchies offer one way to achieve that balance. These hierarchies retain many efficiency advantages of hierarchies, but ameliorate many of the shortcomings. In particular, by disseminating power throughout the organization, loose hierarchies avoid the dullness and inertia that can often undermine the vitality of a large company. Loose hierarchies are not the solution for every big company, but where they are appropriate, they can work very well.

The Choice

This, then, is the first of the possible choices for putting more people at the center of an organization: Delegate much more responsibility inside a basically hierarchical structure. The most common way to do this is to delegate most decisions to lower levels in the organization, retaining at higher levels only the right to evaluate the results and reward people accordingly.

Forming a loose hierarchy isn't easy. The people who will make the decisions have to be ready. They must understand the criteria on which they'll be evaluated, and they need access to the right information. These people may need training as well. Some of them may have to find other jobs, because not everyone is capable of making certain decisions, and even people who are capable don't always want to. Perhaps most importantly, as Dennis Bakke said, the people who currently have the power need to be willing to give it up.

CHAPTER FIVE

Harnessing Democracy

WHEN THE MANAGERS of any of the 143 Whole Foods super-markets in North America decide to hire someone, they know their decision is really only a recommendation. Before becoming a perma-nent employee, every job candidate works for a thirty-day trial period in one of the store's departments, such as produce, bakery, or prepared foods, and then the whole departmental team votes on whether to keep the candidate.

The vote is not just a popularity contest. Because team members get a monthly bonus based on their department's labor efficiency, they're motivated to think very carefully about new hires. They know that the people they select will directly affect their own pay.[1]

This simple example illustrates a second way of making decentral-ized decisions: *democracy*. In a democratic group, everyone abides by whatever decision is made by vote of the group.

We're used to democracy in governments, of course. But govern-mental democracy is usually quite limited, existing only at the very top of the organization. In the United States, for example, the people elect a president, but the president runs a largely hierarchical bureaucracy. The people elect senators and representatives who vote on laws, but the enforcement of the laws is left to a hierarchically organized system of government agencies and courts.

We don't usually think of it this way, but most large companies have a surprisingly similar structure. The stockholders elect a board of directors, the board of directors votes on policies, and then the poli-cies are carried out by a hierarchical organization. A key difference, of course, is that the election of corporate boards is only open to owners of the company's stock, and (usually) the more shares you own, the more votes you get.

But what if democratic decision making took place much more broadly in businesses? Such an idea is not entirely new—some companies have experimented with workplace democracy for decades.[2] For the most part, however, these efforts have been like the experiments with political democracy in ancient Athens: successful in limited situations, but not yet a mainstream trend. As communication costs continue their dramatic fall, however, the democratic form of decentralized decision making is becoming feasible in far more places than ever before. Let's look at some examples of what is already happening—and what it portends for the future.

Opinion Polling

Even though the official management ethos of most businesses today remains hierarchical, democracy has been making steady inroads. Because the willing cooperation of employees is so important to a modern company's success, an increasing number of managers essentially run their units as small democracies. Though the managers have the right to make decisions unilaterally, they usually ask for—and follow—the group's opinion. One manager I know ran a medium-sized consulting firm this way. He rarely made a major decision without extensive discussions with everyone involved; his goal was to guide the discussions toward a rough consensus that almost everyone could support.

In some cases, asking employees what they think is not just a nice idea; it's necessary. When employees collectively own a controlling interest in their company, for example, their votes determine who runs the firm in the first place. In large professional partnerships such as law and accounting firms, all the partners vote on who will be their senior managers.

New information technologies enable this kind of democratic decision making on a much larger scale. With inexpensive Web-based polling and other market research techniques, companies can routinely survey employees, as well as customers and other stakeholders, on all kinds of issues: How satisfied are workers with their new benefits program? What features should be in a new product? What new technologies might change our industry?

One of the world's leading management consulting firms regularly asks its employees whether they think their managers act in accordance with the values of the firm. The values, which are widely disseminated in the company, include aspirations like open, honest communication and putting the clients' interests first. The firm takes the results of these surveys so seriously that it's nearly impossible for managers at any level to be promoted unless their team has given them good ratings.[3]

An even more striking example of opinion polling occurred when Hewlett-Packard (HP) proposed to buy Compaq Computer in late 2001. Critical to the success of the merger was the support of HP's 86,000 employees. As an article in the *Wall Street Journal* put it, "[the employees] are key not only as shareholders, but as the people on the ground who have to make the complex job of integrating Compaq work."[4] The article also reported that HP "has been surveying employees periodically to gauge feelings about the acquisition and . . . the last survey . . . showed that 'a significant majority of employees' support the deal." Today, a story about a major company's polling its employees on a key strategic decision is newsworthy. In the future, it may be the norm.

Participative Decision Making at W. L. Gore

We're also beginning to see a much more extensive use of democratic decision making in business, some involving formal voting and some not. W. L. Gore and Associates, a $1.2 billion company with about six thousand employees, is best known as the maker of Gore-Tex waterproof fabric. But it's also well known for its extremely innovative management style.[5] The company has been named one of *Fortune* magazine's 100 Best Companies to Work for in America every year, from 1998 to 2003.

Other than the president and secretary of the company—two titles required by law for incorporation purposes—no one at Gore has a job title. Everyone is just called an associate. To become a manager, you don't get promoted; you have to go out and find other employees who will agree to work with you. Here's how Terri Kelly, an associate at Gore, explains her role as a team leader: "Although I'm a business leader for military fabric, I'm a leader only if there are people who are willing to follow me. A project doesn't move forward unless people buy into it. You cultivate followership by selling yourself, articulating your ideas, and developing a reputation for seeing things through. . . . Let's say I've come up with a design for a winter sleeping bag for the military. I'd go to the person responsible for marketing the bag and find out whether there's demand for it. If there isn't, I'd go back and try to reposition the plan. If he's excited by the idea and thinks it's viable, I'd bring him in on the project to help me develop it."[6]

In general, decisions are made by this kind of informal consensus building, not by managerial decree. Even salary decisions are made by committees, which draw heavily on written reviews and numerical rankings by employees' peers. "The idea is that employees are not accountable to the president of the company; they're accountable to their colleagues," says Kelly.[7]

The result of all this participative decision making is an extremely happy and creative workforce. In one survey, 97 percent of Gore associates said the company was a great place to work.[8] And even though Gore has no formal R&D department, ideas from associates have helped the company turn out innovative new products year after year.

Cross-Organizational Democracy at Visa International

Democratic decision making structures can be used across organizations as well as within them. Consider the situation faced in the late 1960s by Bank of America and the other banks it had licensed to use its BankAmericard credit card.[9] Operational problems were plaguing the banks as they tried to expand the fledgling business of granting flexible credit to vast numbers of consumers. Bank of America blamed the licensees for many of the problems, and the licensees blamed Bank of America. As the bickering continued, loan losses mounted rapidly.

The banks involved, including Bank of America, were competitors, and none wanted a critical part of its business to be controlled by a rival. But they all had to cooperate—to some degree—for the complex network of banks, merchants, and consumers to operate effectively.

What could they do?

The solution they eventually adopted was a cross-organizational democracy. They created and shared ownership of a for-profit membership corporation. Members had voting rights proportional to their sales volume, although for decisions made by the board of directors, no bank had more than one vote. Votes as high as 80 percent were required to ratify major decisions like changing the name of the card. Bank of America was a member of the new organization, but it was subject to the same rules to which all the other members were subject.

The corporation, which eventually came to be called Visa International, did not issue any cards or make any loans itself. Its only role was to establish the standards, marketing programs, and technology infrastructure to help its member banks collaborate more effectively. And it has succeeded. In the three decades since the corporation was formed, Visa has become one of the most widely recognized brands in the world. By 2002, the Visa network included more than 21,000 member financial institutions in more than 150 countries, and it processed payments for more than $2.4 trillion of goods and services.[10]

Could such success have happened with a more conventional hierarchical organization? It seems unlikely. When the activities of many independent companies—some of which compete with one another—need to be coordinated, a cross-organizational democracy like the one used by Visa (and also by its primary competitor, MasterCard) becomes very attractive.

---

eBay: An Online Democracy for Customers

The examples we've seen so far in this chapter show how businesses can make democratic decisions without any special information technology. But with new technologies, democratic decisions are becoming feasible in many more situations.

Take eBay, the hugely successful Internet auction company. As Fred Reichheld, the author of *Loyalty Rules*, pointed out to me, some of the most important decisions about how the eBay site works are made democratically.[11] There are no official votes, but eBay managers use all kinds of electronic tools to constantly solicit and respond to the opinions of buyers and sellers. When the site first opened, founder Pierre Omidyar encouraged customers to express their opinions via e-mail and an online bulletin board. Today, eBay has dozens of online discussion boards about virtually every aspect of its site and the online communities it has created. When the company is considering making a change in its auctions, it usually posts notices in advance, giving users plenty of time to respond.

In one sense, of course, this is just good marketing. Any well-run company should try to figure out and respond to what its customers want. But eBay does this to such an extent that it often feels like the customers are actually in charge. When, for instance, eBay's senior manager of community strategy, Mary Lou Song, tried to change the color of the stars used to indicate seller ratings on the site, she was surprised at the intensity of the response. "I got flamed by the users for two weeks straight. There were hundreds of messages," she said. Users' comments ranged from "Why did you pick those colors?" to "Do you have any idea how this place works?"[12]

"I kept thinking, 'No, I should be able to figure out what is best for the user base.' It was just stars. But the harder I dug my heels in, the harder the user community would push back."[13]

Eventually, she changed her strategy and began to actively solicit feedback before making changes. Now, she usually won't proceed with a change until most users who participate in the online discussions agree to it: "What you see now is the result of a coordinated effort between the company and the user community. . . . It is a process we follow every day. If there is a problem that we need to fix, we go through it together, creating these feedback loops that people can participate in before we ever hard-code anything in."[14]

This kind of online democracy has worked extremely well for eBay. Since its founding in 1995, it has been one of the fastest-growing U.S. companies. By 2002, it had more than 60 million registered users around the world, revenues of $1.2 billion, and an operating profit margin of more than 30 percent.[15] One of the contributors to this remarkable success is the way eBay's online democracy helps stimulate the energy, creativity, and sense of ownership of a vast community.

Mondragon Cooperative Corporation

One of the most dramatic examples of democracy in business today can be found near the town of Mondragon in the Basque region of Spain, where a remarkable group of more than 150 companies forms the Mondragon Cooperative Corporation (MCC). Many of the member companies are in various manufacturing industries—auto parts, household goods, buses, industrial equipment, and machine tools—but the corporation also includes a bank, a supermarket chain, and a management consulting firm. In total, MCC encompasses about 60,000 employees and in 2001 had revenues of about $8 billion (excluding the bank), making it the seventh largest company in Spain.[16]

Decision-Making Structure

Each of the companies in the Mondragon group is itself a worker-owned cooperative. Almost all employees who have been with one of these cooperatives for more than a few years are "members" of the cooperative. As part owners, the employees of each company are the ultimate decision makers. In other words, instead of having power and authority come down from the top of the hierarchy, it comes up from the bottom. As in most democratic governments, however, the members usually exercise their authority through elected representatives.

The most important of these representatives are the members of the governing councils of the different cooperatives. The councils, which are typically made up of seven to ten employees elected for rotating four-year terms, act as a kind of board of directors for each cooperative. The council hires and fires the cooperative's managing director (equivalent to a CEO), approves the distribution of profits, and votes on other major policy decisions.[17] In addition to electing representatives to the governing council, employees are also entitled to attend twice-yearly general assemblies in which major issues facing the company are discussed and, sometimes, voted on.

The 150 cooperatives are grouped into twenty-two industry sectors, which in turn are grouped into nine divisions. These nine divisions, together with some corporate-level staff groups, make up the MCC.

Each industry sector has its own governing council, managing director, and general assemblies, as does the MCC as a whole. The corporate-level version of the governing council (called the standing committee) elects the president of the MCC and monitors the performance of the senior management team.

In this bottom-up structure, the overall corporation doesn't own its "subsidiary" companies. Just the opposite is true: The individual cooperatives own the corporation. The job of the corporate center is to provide services to the individual cooperatives—the member companies are, in essence, its customers. Any cooperative can leave the MCC if it decides it is no longer receiving adequate value from the corporate managers.

Financial Structure

The unusual decision-making structure of MCC is complemented by an equally unusual financial structure. To become a member-owner of a cooperative, an employee must make an initial capital contribution, equal to approximately half an average annual salary. Typically, the cooperative loans an employee some or all of this amount. Over time, the employee's capital account grows in two primary ways. First, interest accrues on the capital contribution. Second, the employee gets a share (proportional to his or her salary) of the company's profits each year. The money in a capital account cannot actually be used, however, until the employee retires or quits. Instead, it is used by the company as a reserve fund and a source of investment capital. In fact, in years when the cooperative has a loss rather than a profit, the capital accounts decrease. The cooperatives also have rules requiring them to allocate certain proportions of their profits, before any distribution to employees. These funds are allocated to build up their own reserve funds, to share with the other cooperatives and the overall corporation, and to support social and educational activities.

Together, these conservative financial policies help the cooperatives achieve one of their main nonfinancial goals: stable, long-term employment for their members. Over their nearly fifty-year history, the Mondragon companies have weathered significant economic downturns without, for the most part, reducing overall employment. Even when individual cooperatives have gone out of business or had to lay people off, their employees have usually been reassigned to other co-operatives within MCC.

Another of the Mondragon financial policies promotes MCC's goal of creating an egalitarian, cooperative community. Unlike many large companies, which pay their CEOs as much as five hundred times more than what their lowest-paid workers receive, MCC limits the ratio of the salary of the highest-paid worker to that of the lowest-paid to no more than six.[18] In general, this means that lower-level workers are paid more than what they would receive in comparable jobs in other companies, while senior managers receive somewhat less. In my discussions with the people at MCC, however, I got the impression that most employees do not consider this leveling-out of senior manager compensation a major factor. When profit-sharing contributions are taken into account, the shortfalls for senior managers are usually not very large. Furthermore, management jobs at MCC appear to be regarded as high-status positions in the Basque community.

Lessons of Mondragon

Employee-owned companies are not unusual. Many professional services partnerships have been owned by (some of) their employees for decades. And even at some large corporations, like United Parcel Service (UPS), Publix Supermarkets, and United Airlines, the majority of stock is in the hands of the rank and file.[19] All such companies have a potential advantage in attracting and motivating their employees.

But MCC goes much further. First, about 80 percent of the workers in most Mondragon companies are members (and thus owners) of the cooperative—a far higher percentage than in most professional services partnerships. Second, each member of a Mondragon cooperative has only one vote in company decisions; votes are not proportional to the number of shares the person owns or the size of his or her capital account. Perhaps most important, MCC has developed a complex hierarchical structure for organizing large numbers of people and resources, with separate but interlinked representative democracies operating at many levels.

When there is just one level of representative democracy—for example, when employees collectively elect the board of directors for a whole corporation—the decision-making power of individual employees is diluted and may have little motivational effect. But when people can actively participate as decision makers in groups small enough to matter to them (most Mondragon cooperatives have fewer than 1,500 or 2,000 members), the benefits of democratic decision making are greatly amplified.

MCC shows that a large industrial company can be organized not primarily to maximize financial returns for its investors, but to achieve a range of financial and nonfinancial goals that are important to its members. For MCC, the goals include employment stability, regional economic development, and social responsibility.

Would such a structure work in other companies? Certainly, the Basque region's distinctive history and social and cultural environment have contributed to the success of MCC. But worker-owned and democratically controlled companies are also flourishing in other settings. The MCC example reveals that this basic idea can be taken to a new level of complexity, with representative democracies at many different hierarchical levels.

According to the MCC managers with whom I talked, a democratic structure makes management harder in some ways and easier in others. Management is harder because, on top of all the usual skills managers need, you also need an additional set of political and interpersonal skills to manage people who are, in a certain sense, your boss. But management is also easier because all the members of the organization are also its owners—they are each at the center of the organization. Everyone thus has a strong financial and psychological motivation to help the company be as successful as possible—to work hard, to always look for ways to do things better, and to share information that can help the company improve. In many situations, as any manager will tell you, that kind of employee motivation makes the difference between success and failure.

A Radically Democratic Hierarchy

How far could this notion of democracy in business go? In the spirit of stimulating your thinking, let's imagine how a new kind of organization—a radically democratic hierarchy—might work. This scenario is inspired by a Web posting by David Wooley, one of the pioneers of computer conferencing. It also draws on the Mondragon example and the work of the MIT Initiative on Inventing the Organizations of the 21st Century.[20]

Decision Structure

Like the Mondragon cooperatives, this new organization uses a conventional-looking hierarchy to collect information and make decisions and places the source of power at the bottom of the hierarchy rather than the top. But instead of having democratically elected representatives at only three levels—cooperative, industry sector, corporation—every hierarchical level is its own direct democracy. That is, at each level, the members of a group elect their own manager, who also represents them at the next level up. Group members can delegate some or all of their decisions to their manager, but they retain the right to overrule or replace the manager at any time.

Rather than establishing strict rules for representative democracy, as at MCC, each group chooses how to make its own decisions, with a majority vote ultimately deciding any question that can't be resolved by consensus or some other method. The groups are also free to add or remove members as they see fit. In higher-level groups, the votes each manager controls are proportional to the number of people he or she represents. Thus, managers representing large groups have more influence than those representing small ones, and the total number of votes at each level is equal to the number of people represented at that level. In principle, the members of any lower-level group could exercise their voting rights directly as individuals in higher-level groups. In practice, however, most people would probably want to delegate this right to their elected representatives.[21]

Approval Voting

One particularly interesting way for the groups to elect their representatives is through *approval voting*. In approval voting, you can vote for as many candidates as you want. If, for example, you really don't care who represents your group, you could vote for everyone in the group. Or if you felt that any of three people were acceptable, you could vote for all three. The winning candidate is the one with the most approval votes. (Any winning candidate who didn't want the job could, of course, decline, and the candidate with the next highest number of approval votes would then be eligible.)

In principle, approval voting can be continuous; that is, people can change their votes at any time. Whenever the approval rating of the current manager falls below that of someone else in the group, then the other person is given the chance to take over. In practice, however, it's probably desirable to introduce some delays in this process in order to avoid constant disruption—the current manager's approval ratings might have to stay down for six months or a year, say, before a new manager takes over. While all this voting could take place with face-to-face meetings and paper ballots, it all becomes much easier and more feasible when done online or with other electronic tools.

Money Flow

In order to be more than just a collection of independent businesses, the overall organization of this radically democratic hierarchy has the authority to redistribute income received by any of its parts. For instance, the top-level management group (representing everyone in the organization) might decide to move money from mature cash-cow products to promising new ones.

In general, this top-level group (let's call it the executive committee) will simply divide the money among its constituent parts, which will, in turn, divide it again and again all the way down to the lowest-level groups in the organization. The executive committee might, for example, redistribute money to the three different product divisions in the company (let's call them A, B, and C) as well as to several cross-product functions (e.g., sales, finance, and legal). The executive committee will also pay any of its direct expenses not attributable to lower-level groups (dividends, interest, taxes, rent, salaries for executive assistants, consultants' fees, etc.).

To maintain the bottom-up incentives in this organization, most groups will want to determine their own managers' compensation directly rather than having it determined by the higher-level group. For instance, the executive committee determines how much money goes to the sales group overall, but the committee does not determine the specific salary of the head of sales. Instead, the sales group allocates its own manager's salary out of the overall amount it receives. In this way, managers will be strongly motivated to keep the people they represent happy—not just to keep their jobs, but to influence the size of their paycheck.

Determining Compensation

One particularly interesting issue is how group members decide one another's compensation. Some groups may vote on their manager's compensation and then let the manager decide everyone else's pay. Another, more interesting possibility is to let each person in the group assign a percentage of the total compensation budget to all the others. The average of these numbers then determines each person's actual compensation. Some groups may choose to make the votes and the final compensation numbers public; others may keep them secret. The same basic procedure can also be used in higher-level groups whose members need to allocate pools of money to the budgets of the lower-level groups they represent.

The energy company AES has tested a somewhat similar system that sets salaries through peer review. In the experiment, each person sent a proposed salary for himself or herself to everyone else in the group. In a meeting, the entire group revised the individual salaries until they added up to the group's total salary budget. In one case, most people's initial proposals were quite similar, but one man's was way out of line. After about three days of talks, he noticed that the difference between the total of all the proposed salaries and the salary budget was almost equal to the amount his salary was out of range. So he lowered his proposal, and the problem was solved.[22]

Reorganizing and Laying Off People

What happens when a group believes that it needs to reorganize a component group or even lay off people? These decisions are made just like all the others. If the majority of the representatives of a large group decides that part of the group should be reorganized or downsized, that is what happens. Would a large group make such a decision casually? Certainly not. Since the whole management structure represents the interests of its workers, the organization would almost always be reluctant to eject some of its own members. In some cases, though, the good of the whole group might require such a move.

Stockholders

The most consistent way to think about stockholders in this organization is as another group that reports directly to the executive committee. Like any other group, the stockholders provide something of value (investment capital) and, in return, receive compensation (dividends) and voting rights. There are two important differences, however, between the stockholder group and all other groups. First, the financial compensation that stockholders receive may be contractually specified in advance rather than determined periodically by vote of the top group. For example, stockholders might automatically receive a fixed percentage of earnings every year. Second, each individual stockholder does not necessarily receive one vote (as each employee does). Instead, the overall number of votes held by stockholders can be negotiated between the management (representing all the employees) and the stockholders, and then each individual stockholder receives a share of these votes, depending on the amount of stock owned.

A key question is whether the stockholders, collectively, have more than 50 percent of the votes in the top group. If they do, then they could essentially overrule any decisions made by the employees and management. In this case, the whole company becomes a more conventional kind of organization, with ultimate power flowing from the top down. More interesting, therefore, is the situation in which all the stockholders together have less than 50 percent of the votes in the top group. In this case, the stockholders would receive financial compensation and have a voice in running the company, but they would not have the ultimate power that we usually associate with ownership.

Would any stockholders be willing to invest on these terms? It certainly seems possible. Many Wall Street analysts, for example, considered the AES management philosophy (of giving lots of decision-making power to low-level employees) a significant risk factor for the company. But AES turned in stellar investment returns for most of the years since it went public in 1991.[23]

Democracies: Definition

Communication Structure

How Are Decisions Made?

Voting (majority, two-thirds majority, consensus, etc.)

Scope of Decision Making

You must abide by any decision made by a group to which you belong.

Incentives

Vote for what you think is best (either for the group or for you).

The new organizational structure described here goes much further than even AES and Mondragon do in giving power to employees. It genuinely turns the traditional power structure upside down. If this approach unleashes the talents of its people as effectively as it might, then many investors would be eager to have a piece of the action—whether they have ultimate control or not!

Lessons About Democracies

As summarized in the boxes, democracies allow anyone to share information with anyone else, but require everyone to obey the decisions made by the group, whether they agree with those decisions or not. Democracies are, therefore, a kind of intermediate structure between controlled hierarchies and open markets.

Since people in democracies have a say in all the decisions that affect them, they generally have a greater sense of autonomy (and thus creativity and motivation) than in hierarchies. But since the members of a

---

Democracies: Evaluation

Strengths

• Individuals can participate in making all decisions that affect them.
• Group decisions can force individuals to do things for the overall good, even when the individuals might not have chosen to do so on their own.

Weaknesses

• Group usually requires a lot of communication so that voters are well enough informed to vote intelligently.
• Everyone's opinions count equally in making decisions, even when some people are much more qualified to make the decisions than others.

---

democracy have to abide by the decisions, even when they don't agree with them, they have less autonomy than in a market, where people are free to do whatever they want, regardless of the majority opinion. At times, some small groups of employees in democracies may come to feel disenfranchised by larger blocs, and their motivation may be undermined.

Democracies are generally better than markets at resolving difficult conflicts of interest among individuals. That's because democracies can force individuals to do things for the overall good of the group. In our radically democratic scenario, for instance, the executive committee can take income from a mature business and invest it in a promising new business, even if the mature business would never have agreed to this on its own.

The primary disadvantages of democracies result from their relative inefficiency in decision making. Decisions generally require more time, discussion, and effort than in a hierarchy. Furthermore, since everyone's vote counts equally, people who don't understand the issues very well sometimes determine the outcomes. It is easy to imagine dysfunctional versions of the radically democratic scenario. For instance, people may spend too much time politicking, or good—but unpopular—choices don't get made, or particularly divisive issues may disrupt the company for longer than they would in a hierarchy or a market.

The Choice

We've now seen the second major way of putting more people at the center of an organization: Instead of having someone in charge make decisions, you can let everyone in a group vote. We take this way of democratic decision making for granted in our political affairs, but for the most part, it stops at the factory gates. Now you know it doesn't have to stop there.

Even though democracy is not appropriate everywhere in business, new technologies make it much more feasible in many more situations. When it works well, a democratic approach can significantly increase employees' energy, creativity, and sense of ownership in their organization.

But democracy is still not the most extreme kind of decentralization. In the next two chapters, we'll see how markets can sometimes give people even more freedom.

CHAPTER SIX

Unleashing Markets

ONE OF THE CROPS my father grew on our farm was cotton. After it was picked, he would take it to a cotton gin, which he and several other farmers in the area owned cooperatively. From there, the cotton passed through a network of buyers, merchants, and warehouses, with most of it eventually arriving at textile mills in the United States or abroad. The mills spun the cotton into many kinds of cloth, which manufacturers used to produce sheets and shirts, curtains and carpets, toys and towels—all of which ended up being sold to people all over the world.

Who was in charge of this remarkably complex, flexible, and efficient process? No one.

The farmers, mills, apparel makers, distributors, and retailers were all separate entities, and no central authority coordinated their interactions. Whenever two entities agreed on a purchase or sale, they completed the transaction on their own. No further review or approval was needed. No boss told my father how much cotton he had to plant. No outsiders told the cotton mills how much cloth to die blue, and no one told the shirt manufacturers how many long-sleeved men's dress shirts they had to make. In a sense, every player in this very complex process was at the center of the whole process.

The system I've just described is, of course, a market, and today we take for granted its almost miraculous ability to provide us with a broad selection of affordable goods and services. We're no longer surprised at how a myriad of seemingly independent transactions combine to result in an efficient and flexible use of resources.

But we usually don't think about markets as an alternative way to coordinate the business tasks we do in hierarchical companies. Why not? Why can't power, ownership, and initiative be distributed through-out a whole market, rather than being imposed from the top of a hier-archy? Why do we always need to have managers in control? Might not some business tasks be done just as well, or better, if they were guided by the decentralized decisions of many people in a market? And wouldn't people be much more motivated if they had the freedom to make their own choices?

Market structures can be and are being used by companies to or-ganize work. In this chapter, we'll talk about one approach: outsourc-ing tasks to other companies or people through external markets, rather than doing them internally. In chapter 7, we'll talk about a sec-ond—and more surprising—approach: creating internal markets within a single company.

An "E-Lance" Economy

The idea of using outsiders to accomplish certain tasks is nothing new in business. Rather than hiring permanent employees to write and produce marketing brochures, for example, some companies contract with freelance writers and graphic designers to do the work. Instead of making all the subcomponents of their products, many manufacturers routinely buy parts from suppliers. Instead of using in-house depart-ments to manage a benefits program or install a new computer system, some companies outsource such assignments to other companies.

But what if this practice were to expand enormously—to the point where a network of dispersed suppliers replaced the central company al-together? What if, in other words, many tasks currently done by large companies were done instead by temporary combinations of small com-panies and independent contractors? Taking this idea even further, what if most businesses consisted of only a single person? In 1998, my col-league Rob Laubacher and I coined the term *e-lancer*—a term denoting an electronically connected freelancer—to describe this way of working.[1]

In an e-lance economy, the fundamental unit is not the corporation, but the individual. Tasks are not assigned and controlled through a stable chain of management, but rather are carried out autonomously by independent contractors. These freelancers join together into fluid and temporary networks to produce and sell goods and services. When the job is done—after a day, a month, a year—the network dissolves, and its members become independent agents again, circulating through the economy, seeking the next assignment.

This way of organizing is already common in some industries. Perhaps the best-known example is Hollywood. A producer, a director, actors, camera operators, lighting technicians, and other specialists—many of whom are independent contractors—come together for the purpose of making a single film. After it's in the can, they disband and eventually regroup in other combinations for other projects.

The construction industry is often organized this way, too. Plumbers, electricians, carpenters, and other specialists, many of whom work independently or for small companies, join together to make a building. When the building is finished, they regroup in different ways to make other buildings.

Similar organizational structures are becoming common in other, more conventional industries as well. Many information technology projects, for instance, are outsourced to teams of consultants and contractors. Whole new industries are even growing up to do business process outsourcing. These businesses handle entire functions—such as human resource management, accounting, or customer service—on behalf of client companies. The trend is reflected in employment statistics. By a conservative estimate, more than one quarter of the U.S. workforce in 2003 were freelancers of one type or another.[2] This figure leaves out people who work for consulting firms and other organizations that use temporary project teams.

Again, falling communication costs make freelancing and outsourcing more practical. By reducing the transaction costs of finding, selecting, working with, and paying people for a project, new communication technologies make it easier to organize temporary teams.[3] And the freedom of this e-lance way of working holds great appeal for many people.

Benefits and Limitations of Freelancing

The freelance way of organizing can be extremely flexible and efficient for businesses. Companies (or departments within companies) don't need large staffs of specialists on hand all the time. Instead, they can assemble teams only when needed, and each team can include precisely the right combination of skills and people for the task at hand. If it's worth the cost, companies can even bring in the best people available in the world—not just the ones who happen to be on staff.

Freelancing is not right for every business. Some companies must keep groups of employees together over long periods in order to solve difficult problems or carry out complex projects. Other companies' needs are so stable that the extra flexibility provided by organizing teams of e-lancers would not be worth the cost. But as business continues to require greater flexibility and as new technologies reduce the cost of providing it, more and more of our economy will become an e-lance economy—one in which every worker is at the center of a complex web of ever-shifting, interconnected processes.

Such a shift will be attractive to many workers. They can choose when, where, and how they want to work, which means they can bring their own personal values more directly into their business decision making. Working mothers and fathers can build their work schedules around their child-care responsibilities. Older workers can create portfolios of projects to help them stay active and earn extra income. People with diverse interests can arrange mini-sabbaticals for themselves without needing the authorization of a corporate policy. Those so inclined can donate substantial amounts of their time to charitable causes. And those who want to work eighty-hour weeks for some periods of their lives can be well compensated for doing that, too.

Not all people desire or need the flexibility and autonomy that freelancing provides. Some would prefer working in a stable corporate environment. And, as we'll see later in this chapter, many fear leaving the corporate nest—they know that there's currently a lack of support structures for independent contractors. Freelancing has other risks as well.[4] When you're getting paid by the hour or job rather than drawing a regular salary, you may let your work absorb more and more of the time you might otherwise have spent with your family or on other activities. But if you're clear about your values and have the self-discipline to live by them, freelancing gives you the flexibility to do so.

Elance, Inc.

In an e-lance economy, people are continually being grouped and regrouped into project teams. Doing this well requires a lot of information: What needs to be done? What kinds of skills are needed to do it?

Who is available? How good are they? How much do they charge? In a small community, it's easy to exchange such information informally. But for an e-lance economy to work well on a large scale, an infrastructure for exchanging information is essential. Since the late 1990s, a number of companies have been emerging to provide exactly this kind of infrastructure using the Internet.

My favorite example is Elance, Inc.[5] The basic idea of the Elance Web site is to create online auctions for a wide range of professional services—software development, graphic design, market research, language translation, and so on. All the services have one important thing in common: They can be performed electronically, without the buyer and the seller ever having to meet face-to-face. By fall 2001, Elance had more than 400,000 registered users from more than 160 countries around the world.

To use the site, a buyer posts a description of the project and receives bids from many different contractors. Based on the bids (and ratings of the bidders by previous clients), the buyer hires a contractor. When the project is over, both buyer and seller rate each other, and their respective online reputations are updated. For example, I used Elance to have some slides made. I described the project online, and within a day or so, I had received about a dozen bids. I picked what I thought was the best bidder based on her previous experience, as documented in her electronic portfolio and her prior ratings. Within a few days, she had completed the job to my satisfaction.

In the course of doing the slides, I realized that I wanted to make a particular graph about the audiences at two conferences. I was fairly sure of how I wanted the graph to look, but to make it, I needed exact numbers for attendance at the conferences. I spent a while looking on the Web, but couldn't find the information easily. I consequently decided to outsource this research as a separate task on Elance. Again, within a day or so, I had received about six bids, and within another couple of days, I had the chart I needed.

This example shows how the Elance concept can be used, not just for outsourcing the work of an entire company, but also for micro-outsourcing from inside large companies. It wasn't that the entire project (of preparing a talk) was handed over to e-lancers or that my whole company (in this case, MIT) was disbanded. Instead, I just outsourced a couple of small tasks, the preparation of some slides and a bit of research. Thousands of similar tasks are carried out every day in large organizations—tasks that professionals and managers do themselves or delegate to assistants. In many cases, it would make more sense to offload these jobs to a market. But in the past, this small amount of outsourcing wouldn't have been worth the hassle. With the arrival of the Internet, however, it suddenly becomes possible to mobilize markets for even very simple activities.

In fact, since large companies still dominate our economy today, Elance is focusing on helping them manage their procurement of services. Over time, as the infrastructures for e-lancing become more and more refined and the concepts more and more accepted, the boundaries of individual companies may come to matter less and less.

Asynchrony Software

Asynchrony Software, another fascinating example of the e-lance concept, focuses only on making markets for software projects. Its infrastructure is similar to the Linux open-source model, but with an important difference. Linux relies on people writing software just for the love of writing software; they don't actually get paid for their efforts. Asynchrony engages these people's economic motivations, too. The company slogan is "Code for love *and* money."

Here's how it works: Someone with an idea for a software project posts it on the Asynchrony Web site. People interested in working on it respond, and the project leader selects a team. Before work begins, the leader must reach agreement with the team members about how any eventual revenues will be divided among them. In other words, each project is like a small start-up company, with each team member receiving equity in it.

Once the team is formed, development proceeds in a more or less conventional way. Each person writes his or her part of the software, the project leader provides overall guidance, and the code is shared electronically through the site. Interestingly, the "beta testers" who exhaustively test early versions of the software to find bugs are also recruited through the site and receive shares of the revenue. When the software is finished, Asynchrony helps market it, typically receiving between 10 percent and 25 percent of the revenue.

There's no one sitting at the top of Asynchrony telling others, "Here are our priorities: We're going to develop these kinds of software, and we need to hire this many programmers with these kinds of special-ties." Instead, these decisions are decentralized through the Asyn-chrony community of more than thirty thousand people around the world. The individual members and teams decide for themselves what projects to do, who will do them, how to appraise performance, and how to reward contributors.

So far in Asynchrony, projects are initiated only by technologists who have "cool ideas" with commercial potential. A clearly desirable extension of this concept would be to allow companies and other software buyers to initiate projects as well. It would also probably make sense for Asynchrony to expand beyond people with technical skills and allow marketers and other business specialists to get involved.

Finally, the people who currently work on Asynchrony projects re-ceive no immediate compensation—only the promise of a share of fu-ture revenues. That's fine for small projects or for people already sup-porting themselves in other ways. But for some large projects, it would also be desirable to have the equivalent of venture capitalists—people who would underwrite the early stages of development in return for their own share of the eventual revenues.

Whether Asynchrony will be successful remains to be seen. But the advantages of its basic business model are compelling—not just for software development, but also for the creation of many other intellec-tual products, such as textbooks, newspapers, and product designs for physical products. It seems inevitable that this model for organizing work will expand as communication costs continue to fall.

---

eBay

Chapter 5 discussed eBay, the Internet auction company, as an exam-ple of a democracy. But eBay is also a market—a vast global one. In 2003, it racked up more than $5 billion in gross merchandise sales, accounting for 2 percent of all U.S. e-commerce and involving 30 mil-lion active buyers and sellers.[6]

The company didn't grow to its remarkable size in just eight years by hiring lots of retail employees. Instead, the sellers on eBay do the work that would be done by store clerks (and buyers, merchandisers, marketers, and shippers) in a conventional retail company. In effect, eBay provides an infrastructure in which hundreds of thousands of people can work as freelance retailers.

For example, eBay estimates that between 130,000 and 150,000 people are so active as sellers that they make their living on eBay.[7] If these people were all employees of the company, eBay would be one of the fifty largest private employers in the United States.[8] But these eBay peddlers aren't employees; each seller is essentially a self-employed proprietor of his or her own retail store.

What underpins eBay's market—or any market, for that matter—is trust. Establishing trust is especially important on the Internet because, when you're dealing with someone you've never met, in a distant city, with no physical storefront, the usual cues that help you establish trust are missing. eBay pioneered a sophisticated reputation system for solving this problem.[9] After each transaction, the buyer and seller rate each other, and their cumulative ratings are immediately updated for every eBay member to see.

Most eBay participants try very hard to avoid a negative rating for any transaction. They know that their reputation is critical to their future sales. In fact, less than 1 percent of the ratings are negative. Fraud, though it does occasionally occur, affects only an estimated 0.01 percent of all transactions.[10]

eBay is a striking example of one of the central premises of this book. The company uses the inexpensive worldwide communication infrastructure of the Internet to give millions of e-lance retailers the benefits of global scale in marketing and distribution without requiring them to give up the freedom, personalization, and motivation of small-town store owners.

Topsy Tail

A remarkable example of how far outsourcing can go (even without new communication technologies) is a small company called Topsy Tail. Based in Dallas, Texas, this company makes a plastic hairstyling tool for women and girls. In one recent year, its revenues hit $80 million—yet the company had only three employees!

Topsy Tail lets contractors do almost everything; the company never once touches its own product as it passes through the supply chain. The device is made by injection-molding contractors, which ship it directly to fulfillment houses, which in turn ship it to sales reps and distributors. About all that Topsy Tail's staff does is develop new products and plan marketing strategy. By using a decentralized, market-based structure, the company has grown much faster and become more flexible than it could have if Topsy Tail had to build its own factories, warehouses, and distribution centers.

One reason Topsy Tail has been able to rely so heavily on outsiders is that it holds a patent on its product. As a result, the company doesn't have to worry about suppliers making copycat goods. (Protecting intellectual property needs to be a key consideration for any company looking to open its doors to broader markets.) Nevertheless, Topsy Tail's success shows that it is possible to supplant a traditional corporate organization with a flexible web of small companies.

The Prato Textile Industry

The textile industry near Prato, Italy, is an example of a different kind of decentralized market. Starting in the mid-1970s, the big textile companies that used to dominate production in the region began to break apart. By 2000, there were more than fifteen thousand small firms, which averaged fewer than five employees. These are not primitive, cottage-industry businesses—the firms use state-of-the-art equipment. And to enjoy economies of scale, the companies have cooperative ventures for functions like purchasing and R&D.

What ties the system together is a group of brokers, known as *impannatori,* who help the small companies work together. When an incoming order is too big for any one company to handle, the brokers put together a temporary coalition, or consortium, to fill it.

But while the brokers facilitate the market, they don't control it. There's no CEO of the Prato textile industry. Every party makes its own decisions about whom to do business with and on what terms. Out of all these decentralized interactions comes some of the best fashion material in the world.

The Internet

The Internet itself has a market structure, and its main commodity is information. "Sellers" decide what kind of information to make available (and whether to charge for it, use it to advertise some other product or service, or just give it away), and "buyers" decide if they want to use it (and, if necessary, pay for it). Most buyers and sellers also pay some kind of access fee to be connected to the Internet—to enter the market, in other words.

As in most markets, everyone on the Internet is, in a sense, at its center. There's no one in charge—no one who can shut the Net down, no one who can block access or control transactions. In fact, the Internet can be considered simply a set of interaction protocols—rules for exchanging information. Anyone who follows those protocols can play whatever role he or she wants—network provider, service provider, or service user.

Paradoxically, the rigid technical standards at one level (what is called the Internet Protocol, or IP) enable all the amazing flexibility of the Internet at the other levels. Because everyone obeys the overarching standards, people can build lots of different capabilities at different levels, and all these capabilities can work together.

In addition to the standards, a few crucial, centrally managed processes, like the establishment of top-level domain names (.com, .edu, .biz, etc.) help the Internet run smoothly. The processes are supervised by a set of elected and volunteer boards, such as the Internet Engineering Task Force (IETF) and the Internet Corporation for Assigned Names and Numbers (ICANN). Though these basic processes are sometimes contentious (there are continuing debates about how many new domain names should be created), they require only a minuscule fraction of the effort that would be needed to manage such an incredibly complex system in a more centralized way.

One illustrative experiment is to imagine that some large, centralized organization had been running the Internet. I have heard, for instance, that AT&T was twice offered the chance to run it, and both times declined. What would have happened if Ma Bell had said yes? Do you think the Internet could have grown as far and as fast as it has (doubling its size in most years since 1988)? We can't know for sure, of course, but when I ask most people this question, they shake their heads in disbelief. They think that the explosive growth of the Internet could never have happened under Ma Bell's oversight.

Maybe there really is some deep tie between the unusually decentralized nature of the Internet and its amazing growth, flexibility, and innovativeness. What if we could somehow harness this kind of energy for other kinds of business purposes? Just think how much intelligence, energy, and creativity we might unleash!

Too Much Freedom?

So far in this chapter, we've seen intriguing examples of how you can use markets in surprising—and powerful—ways. But what about the people in these markets? What do they want?

When I talk about using markets rather than traditional companies to organize work, people sometimes get nervous. They say, "But not everyone wants this much freedom. Some people just want to be told what to do, so they can do their job and go home to their families and to the other parts of their lives that really matter to them." And, of course, this is true. Not everyone wants more autonomy. And not everyone who wants more autonomy is capable of handling it well.

You can think of the people in any community as being arrayed along a spectrum measuring the degree of autonomy they want and can handle. If this distribution is typical of most things in the world, it will form a normal curve (figure 6-1).

FIGURE 6-1

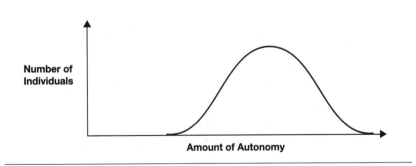

FIGURE 6-2

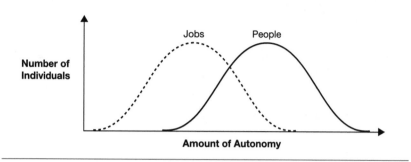

Now, if you were also to graph the amount of autonomy needed and allowed in the jobs in the same community, you would see another distribution. In most places today, the two distributions probably wouldn't match up (figure 6-2). In other words, there are probably still more people who want and can handle more autonomy in their work than there are jobs that provide it.

What we should work toward is a world in which the two curves line up. We don't want or need everyone to have complete autonomy. That would just leave lots of people adrift with more choices than they could deal with. To take real advantage of the true potential of many people, however, we need to provide many more opportunities for autonomous action. And this is exactly what new, more decentralized organizations will do.

Taking Care of People: The Guilds of the Future

The decentralized organizations we've been talking about give people much more freedom and flexibility. Freelancers have many more choices, for example, about where, when, how, and on what they work. But what about their other needs—for financial security, for health care, for socializing with peers, for recognition, for training? Once they're on their own, how will workers gain access to such necessities? And how will they acquire a sense of identity in a world of ever-shifting alignments?

Until recently, the implicit employment contract in traditional corporations provided clear answers to these questions. Workers gave loyal service to their employers and, in exchange, received job security, health insurance and pensions, a chance for career advancement, and, in many cases, even a kind of extended family. This arrangement marked a significant advance over the more primitive working conditions of the early industrial age, but it was itself a product of its time— the mid-twentieth century. Since about the 1980s, business conditions have changed. Workers have become more mobile, less tethered to a single company. And buffeted by competition, most companies have abandoned any promise of lifetime employment. In many cases, people expect to spend no more than a few years, or even a few months, at any one company.

As this trend continues, we'll need to find ways to replace the security and services embedded in the old employment contract. If we don't, we'll be in danger of creating a lonely and unpleasant world, where workers' human needs go unfulfilled.

One particularly promising approach has emerged from our work at MIT. As we thought about the challenge, we realized that there was an obvious, but not yet widely recognized, solution. Rather than relying on employers and governments to provide the benefits traditionally associated with a job, a new set of organizations might emerge to provide stable "homes" for mobile workers and to look after their needs as they move from job to job and project to project.

These organizations might be called societies, associations, fraternities, or clubs. But the word I like best is *guilds,* a term that conjures up images of the craft associations of the Middle Ages. Growing out of tradesmen's fraternities and mutual assistance clubs, medieval guilds served a number of functions: They trained apprentices and helped them find work. They cemented social bonds—guild members worshipped together and marched as a group in town pageants. They offered loans and schooling. And if misfortune struck, they provided an income for members' families.[11]

What Can Guilds Do?

Existing organizations already perform some of these functions today. Take the Screen Actors Guild. As much as 30 percent of the base pay of

Screen Actors Guild members goes to the guild's benefits fund. In return, members get full health benefits (even in years when they have no work), generous pensions, and professional development programs.

Imagine an extended version of this arrangement, in which members pay a fraction of their income to a guild in good times in return for a guaranteed minimum income in bad times. Unlike conventional unemployment insurance, provided through a distant, impersonal bureaucracy, the unemployment benefits provided by a guild could go well beyond temporary cash payments. For instance, other guild members would have an incentive—and often the opportunity—to help fellow members find work. A guild would also have the means and the motivation to help its members gain new skills to remain economically productive as times change. Finally, the members would likely exert social pressure on unemployed colleagues who they felt weren't really trying to find work. A faceless bureaucracy could never exert this kind of pressure as effectively.

Another important benefit companies provide for their employees today is simply a place to socialize—at the proverbial water cooler, in meetings, over lunch. When workers are independent contractors, shifting between project teams and often working from home, they may feel isolated. Guilds can help. They can provide places—both physical and electronic—for their members to socialize. Imagine, for instance, a guild that provides always-open "clubhouses" in major cities and that sponsors regular coffees or lunches in smaller towns and neighborhoods.

Companies have also traditionally helped their employees learn skills and, by assigning job titles and other kinds of credentials, signify to the world the capabilities of their workers. These kinds of services could also be provided by guilds. Lawyers and doctors, for instance, have professional societies that establish and monitor the credentials of practitioners and provide continuing educational opportunities. Unions have also had similar functions for years, helping craft workers progress from apprentices to journeymen to master craftsmen.

Finally, many people today derive much of their identity from their employer. "I work for IBM," "I work for Procter & Gamble," or "I work for MIT," people often say as they introduce themselves. If you work for a different organization every week, where will you get this sense of self? Your self-identity could come from your membership in a guild:

"I am a member of the Institute of Electrical and Electronic Engineers," or "I am a member of the MIT Alumni Guild." Arguably, the shared profession of guild members offers a stronger basis for personal identity than does a large and heterogeneous corporation.

How Will Guilds Be Formed?

A variety of existing organizations already fill some of the roles of guilds. Many of them could fairly easily extend their services.

Professional Societies   Many professional societies provide their members with opportunities for insurance, training, and socializing. For example, the Association for Computing Machinery, a society for computer professionals, offers career placement services, medical insurance, life insurance, conferences, publications, a credit card, product discounts, and a lifetime e-mail forwarding service. As more members of professional societies leave permanent corporate jobs, the societies could become the members' new professional homes.

Labor Unions   Today, we usually think of collective bargaining as the primary role of labor unions. But if the large corporations with which unions bargain go away, unions could evolve into guilds, doing much more for their members. After all, unions have long provided portable benefits for workers who move frequently from one employer to another (e.g., in construction and entertainment). Unions have also sometimes provided job referrals (e.g., the union hiring halls of the early 1900s) as well as opportunities for socializing and assistance in times of need. In the future, full-service unions, as my MIT colleague Tom Kochan calls them, might make it their business to provide more extensive services to their members, including job referrals and placement, retraining, and insurance.[12] Some unions, like the AFL/CIO, are already beginning to talk about such possibilities.[13]

The whole dialogue between unions and companies might change. The old dialogue goes something like this:

COMPANIES: *We have to make money.*
UNIONS: *You owe us good jobs.*

Here's what the new dialogue might sound like:

COMPANIES: *How can we meet the changing needs of the market?*
UNIONS: *How can we help our members be economically productive?*

To fulfill broader roles, unions may need to surrender some control. In the past, to bargain effectively with large (and sometimes monopolistic) companies, unions had to maintain their own monopolies over the workers in a given occupation. But if the unions no longer do collective bargaining, they would no longer need monopoly control. In fact, they would probably serve their members better without it. The history of competitive free markets shows that workers would often be better off if they had multiple unions, or guilds, competing to provide them the best services at the best prices.

Temporary Staffing Firms   Today's temp agencies might also evolve into guilds. Already, many of these firms offer benefits that resemble those provided by traditional employers—vacation and sick pay, health insurance and pensions, training, career assistance, even stock options. Aquent Associates, for example, a staffing firm based in Boston, provides not only health, pension, and vacation benefits, but also extensive career assistance. Aquent calls this last service having "your own personal Jerry Maguire," an allusion to the Hollywood movie about an agent who represents professional athletes.

College Alumni Associations   Guilds may also emerge from college alumni associations. Many people feel a strong, lifelong affinity for their colleges and classmates, and many alumni associations already provide some of the services that guilds should provide. The MIT alumni association, for instance, provides career placement assistance, publications, e-mail forwarding, and extensive meetings and educational opportunities. There's no reason why it couldn't become the primary professional home for some of its members.

New Organizations   The guilds of the future may also come from new organizations. For example, in 2003, eBay began offering health insurance to "power sellers," thirty thousand of its most active merchants.[14] And Working Today, a recently launched New York nonprofit, is focusing on supporting the freelance technology workers in Manhattan's Silicon Alley. The organization already offers these workers health insurance, life insurance, disability insurance, and a set of financial services, including retirement account management and no-fee checking accounts. Eventually, Working Today hopes to expand its services to other communities of independent professionals.

Traditional Corporations Even traditional corporations might become guilds. What if companies no longer saw their primary role as directing employees in satisfying customers? What if, instead, they assumed it was the job of individual employees to figure out how to find and serve customers? What if each employee's income depended on how well he or she performed this job? And what if the primary role of the company was just to provide a stable home, and a set of useful services, to help employees do that job well? In fact, what if companies viewed their primary customers as the employees whose work they were supporting?

In some ways, this world might not look all that different from the world we're used to. Many people might still continue to work for the same big companies. But the processes, philosophies, and attitudes of these companies would be 180 degrees different from what they are today.

In any case, whether the needs of individual workers are met by existing organizations with expanded roles, by entirely new organizations, or by transformed versions of large corporations, all of us need to think creatively about how best to take care of independent workers in our increasingly dynamic economy.

The Choice

Now we've seen another major way of putting many people at the center of an organization: Instead of delegating decisions or making decisions by voting, you let the market decide. That is, you let big decisions emerge from many little decisions made by individual buyers and sellers.

In this chapter, we've seen how this can work when legally independent people and companies transact business in an open market. But you can also get many of the benefits of a market *inside* a single company. That's the subject of chapter 7.

CHAPTER SEVEN

Bringing Markets Inside

IN 1998, John Browne, the chairman and CEO of British Petroleum (BP), made a public commitment to reduce the company's greenhouse gas emissions by 10 percent, from 1990 levels, by the year 2010. If your CEO were to set such a goal, how do you think your company would go about achieving it?

Most companies would probably do something like this: Senior managers would establish target reductions for business units, which in turn would set individual targets for each of their plants. Many plants would claim that their targets were unfair and unrealistic, whether they really were or not, and there would be a period of bargaining before final targets were established. As work progressed, some plants would find it easy to meet their targets, and once they had, they would have little incentive to do more. Other plants would have to spend huge amounts of time and money to meet their targets. Sometimes, they might convince their managers to reduce the targets. In other cases, they would give up, and everyone involved would look bad. In the end, some progress would be made, but the process would be inefficient, unpleasant, and divisive.

British Petroleum didn't use this kind of centralized, hierarchical approach at all. Instead, it set up an internal market to coordinate the efforts of the different business units.[1] Here's how it works: First, managers assign targets to business units by handing out a certain number of "permits." Each permit gives the holder the right to make one ton of carbon-dioxide-equivalent emissions a year. Then, the business units buy and sell permits among themselves, using a specially designed electronic trading system. For instance, if one unit head sees a way to exceed his or her reduction target, the manager could sell the extra permits to other business units that are having trouble meeting their targets. In 2001, BP business units traded more than 4.5 million tons of emissions rights using this system, at an average internal price of about $40 per ton.

In this way, all the business unit managers within BP can make their own decisions about the level of emissions reduction that makes sense for them. And BP as a whole gains an efficient way of finding the most cost-effective methods of reducing emissions throughout the entire company. The approach has been so successful that by 2001, BP had already met its original goal of reducing emissions by 10 percent—nine years ahead of schedule!

As this example shows, markets don't always have to be outside a company. You can also use marketlike decision-making methods inside the boundaries of a single company. Sometimes, as in the case of BP, these internal markets involve transfers of real money between different units. But they can also be based on point systems or other informal indications of value.

Companies have experimented for decades with a rough version of this idea called internal transfer pricing—where one part of a company sells products or services to another part of the same company.[2] When it works well, transfer pricing gives managers some of the incentives of a market. But it's a rudimentary method, often subject to politicking or other bureaucratic distortions. Now, however, new technologies are making it easier to manage the complex information exchanges required to operate true markets within companies.

Internal Freelancing

It's now possible, for instance, to set up an internal labor market for assigning employees to projects—to establish, in other words, an e-lance economy within a company. Indeed, companies are realizing that market-based systems can help assure that talent is allocated more efficiently and flexibly than is possible in traditional hierarchies, where people are tied to particular units. Even in large companies, more and more professionals—engineers, marketing specialists, salespeople, consultants, and even managers—are becoming internal freelancers, working on small teams that are constantly forming, shifting, and disbanding as projects come and go. While they may receive a regular paycheck, the internal freelancers are ultimately responsible for selling themselves within the company—repeatedly finding places where they can add value and building a reputation that will make other employees want to work with them.

Venture-funded start-up companies often operate in this manner as well. Small, temporary teams are assembled to do specific tasks (e.g., getting initial funding, developing the first product, or building a sales organization), allowing different sets of skills to be brought in at each stage in a company's development. People move frequently from job to job, depending on their contacts and personal networks. Sometimes, they stay at one company for a couple of years, sometimes for only a few months.[3] Even though they officially work for larger companies, internal freelancers are, in a sense, entrepreneurs, running their own one-person businesses.

Quasi Markets to Form Project Teams

Most internal freelancers depend on informal networking to find work. But some companies are setting up more formal labor markets within their walls. Merck's research division has for a long time given individual researchers a great deal of freedom over which projects they work on.[4] Project leaders don't have budgets or grants of authority from on high; instead they have to recruit their team members, each of whom brings his or her own equipment and other resources to the project. Projects that can't attract a critical mass of talent just don't happen.

Hewlett-Packard is experimenting with an even more elaborate system.[5] Though not exactly a formal market with real money and equity shares like the one used by Asynchrony, HP's system has many of the same structural characteristics. I call it a quasi market, and it works like this: Anyone in HP who has an idea for a new project can propose it to a board of senior managers at what the company calls its VC Café. The board acts as a kind of venture capital group, providing funding to the projects it finds most promising. Descriptions of the approved projects are posted on an internal network, and anyone who is interested in working on a project can let the project leader know. The leader talks to all the candidates and builds a project team.

In this way, skill combinations can be continually changed without the need to constantly restructure the organization. Good ideas percolate up from throughout the organization. Projects find people with the right capabilities, wherever they are in the organization. People find projects that suit them even if their managers don't precisely know their particular interests. And managers get continuing feedback about what projects their people think are most promising. What's more, if the VC Café board finds that no one is interested in doing a project it has approved, it rethinks its decision. If the people who know how to do the work don't think it's interesting, maybe it isn't such a good idea after all!

In one of our MIT research projects, we're working with HP to extend this approach. Two of the most intriguing possibilities we've discussed are a dual hierarchy and an explicit internal market.

A Dual Hierarchy: Project Managers and People Managers

In today's organizations, the same managers are generally responsible for both the tasks done in their groups and the people who do them. In a dual hierarchy, these two responsibilities are separated and assigned to two kinds of managers. *Project managers* are responsible for the tasks—for managing temporary teams of people to achieve specified results. *People managers* are responsible for the people—for helping them find projects that use their skills, enable them to develop and grow as individuals, and bring the greatest overall benefits to the company.

Unlike in traditional organizations, managers in dual hierarchies don't have to make staffing decisions alone. Information technology is used to widely distribute information about what needs to be done and who can do it, enabling team leaders and members to quickly identify and evaluate one another. Communication barriers no longer force workers to stay within the bounds of relatively small units.

Explicit Internal Markets

The HP experiment also raises the possibility of using more explicit market mechanisms. The VC Café review board, for example, might allocate to each approved project a sum of cash that the project leader could use to bid for team members. If a leader thought a particular person was critical to a project, for instance, he or she could use a lot of the budget to bid for that person, even if the project wasn't a very high priority for the company. By the same token, people who wanted to be part of a project or had no other projects to do at the moment might accept lower fees than they usually receive.

Each potential team member, as well as each people manager, would in effect become a profit center, seeking to maximize his or her income. At the end of the year, the profits that team members and people managers had accumulated in their profit centers would affect their pay, their recognition, or other rewards. In this way, everyone is motivated to do whatever is most valuable for the organization at any point in time. And that, of course, is the true goal of human resource management.

Not all organizations will want to go all the way to setting up money-based internal markets. But each organization can choose for itself where it wants to be along the continuum from traditional hierarchies to true markets—and it can alter its position as its needs change. The farther an organization goes along this continuum, the more its employees will feel like entrepreneurs—at the center of their own business.

Idea Futures

Sometimes, internal markets don't involve buying and selling things; they just involve exchanging information. In one recent experiment, HP worked with Caltech economist Charles Plott to create an unusual kind of internal market for information.[6] Its purpose was to collect and distill information scattered throughout the company about the likely future sales of HP printers. But rather than buying and selling the information directly, the participants just bought and sold *predictions* about the future sales. For example, if you thought that the sales in September would be between 1501 and 1600 units, you could buy shares of a kind of futures contract for this prediction. If you were right and sales actually fell within this range, you would get $1.00 for each share you owned. If you were wrong, you would get nothing.

There were contracts for each of ten different sales ranges, and the participants were mostly from the HP sales force. Each person started with about twenty shares in each of the markets. The markets were open for several days, when the participants could buy and sell shares on the basis of their own sense of what the level of sales would be.

The markets ended up predicting the sales of printers even better than the official HP predictions! In sixteen experiments, the sales levels forecast by the market were always at least as close to the actual sales as the official predictions. In all but one case, the market forecasts were significantly closer.

How could this be? Why couldn't the analysts in the central HP sales staff—people whose job it was to predict sales—do a better job than a group of salespeople spending only a few minutes per day for a few days? Quite simply, the central planners don't have all the information that the dispersed salespeople collectively have. Even if the central staff polls the field, lots of biases will affect the answers they receive. One salesperson may want to make his number look big to keep his boss happy until after performance reviews are completed; one sales manager may want to make her number look small so that she can argue that she needs more staff.

In the market, on the other hand, all salespeople are motivated to trade on the basis of what they truly think will happen, not what they want to happen or what they want others to think will happen. Even more importantly, the traders can see the current consensus view of all their colleagues. Then they can use whatever other information they have (even if it's just their instincts) to form a judgment about whether a given prediction at a given price is a good buy.[7]

Robin Hanson first proposed this concept of idea futures in about 1988, and several other people have experimented with it since.[8] For example, the Iowa Electronic Markets Web site has run markets for all U.S. presidential elections since the George Bush–Michael Dukakis contest of 1988.[9] Anyone with access to the Internet can participate, playing with up to $500 of real money. Instead of just having shares that pay off $1.00 to the winner and nothing to the losers, the presidential races also include "vote share" markets. In these markets, the value of a share for George Bush, say, will end up matching the actual percentage of the popular votes he receives.

Remarkably, this electronic market is often more accurate at predicting actual vote proportions than the opinion polls.[10] On the eve of the 1988 election, the Iowa market forecast a vote share for Bush of 53.2 percent, which was exactly right. The market forecast a share for

Dukakis of 45.2 percent, which was only 0.2 percent less than the share he actually received. This was substantially more accurate than any of the opinion polls in that year. Why? As in the HP market, most traders based their bets not on their desires or other ulterior motives, but on a cold assessment of what they really thought would happen. And those who had the most money at stake—and thus the most influence over the market—had the greatest incentive to act rationally.[11]

There are a variety of other idea futures markets on the Internet for predicting everything from movies' box office receipts (www.hsx.com), to stock market prices (www.biz.uiowa.edu/iem), to the emergence of future technologies like self-driving cars (www.ideosphere.com). A research group at MIT is using a similar idea to do market research measuring customer preferences for products that don't exist yet.[12]

Just as this book was going to press, the U.S. Defense Department proposed a similar market for estimating the probabilities of various events related to terrorism in the Middle East. At first, the idea was widely criticized, but then thoughtful observers began to see significant potential in variations of the concept. The proposal was, as one editorial summarized, a "PR disaster," but a very intriguing idea.[13]

One of the reasons idea futures markets aren't more widely used already is that betting on the outcomes of events with real money is illegal in most places. The Iowa Electronic Markets, for instance, has a special "no action" letter from the U.S. Commodity Futures Trading Commission that gives it permission to operate as an educational institution. Such restrictions are nothing new—many of today's widely used financial instruments (like maritime insurance, life insurance, and futures contracts) were once illegal.[14]

Assuming the legal restrictions on idea futures will someday be relaxed, it's not hard to imagine such markets proliferating. Many businesses could incorporate market-based predictions about technological advances, economic conditions, and business changes into their strategic planning—without having to pay anything for the information. (Market analysts good at making predictions might well make more money from trading in these markets than from speaking about and publishing their opinions.) Whether or not public markets emerge, companies will likely follow HP's lead and set up their own internal idea futures markets—to predict their sales, the success of their product development projects, and so forth.

And companies could go even further. What if, instead of just predicting final outcomes (like sales), HP also had internal futures markets for different outcomes based on alternative actions the company might take? For example, what if it had markets for predictions like "If we cancel product line X, our profits next year will increase."

HP might not want to immediately pursue all the actions recommended by the prices in such futures markets. Many senior managers, however, would certainly be very interested in what the informed consensus of people throughout their organization was saying about the future!

Internal Markets for Manufacturing Capacity

One of the most interesting possibilities my colleagues and I have been studying at MIT is the use of internal markets not just for assigning people or collecting information, but for allocating hard assets like manufacturing capacity. In one experiment, we worked with Intel Corporation to create a prototype of an internal market for manufacturing resources.[15]

Like most of today's large and successful manufacturing organizations, Intel uses a complex set of processes to decide how to use its capacity. The processes, which have familiar names like strategic planning, capacity planning, budgeting, factory scheduling, and pricing, are very hierarchical, often cumbersome and inflexible. They consume huge amounts of time, money, and management talent. Many people in the company would say they just aren't flexible enough for the rapidly changing environment.

The key idea we were considering in our experiment was whether capacity could be allocated more effectively through decentralized, marketlike processes. We suspected that a kind of internal market, if implemented well, could result in much more profitable and timely decisions at much lower cost. In particular, we wanted to test the feasibility of a market in which plant managers, sales representatives, and other employees could buy and sell futures contracts for specific products available at specific times in the future. For example, the internal price of one wafer's worth of integrated circuit chips (approximately one hundred actual chips) shipped from Arizona next week might be $80, but the price of the same number of chips shipped from Arizona eight weeks from now might be only $60.[16] Starting with a simple simulation developed by economist David McAdams from our team of MIT and Intel participants, we looked at one product, one plant manager, and five sales representatives.

We used an experimental Web-based market-making system that was developed at MIT and that lets players place buy and sell orders as in the real stock market.[17] You can offer to buy or sell *at market* (that is, at whatever the current market price is), or you can place a limit order to buy or sell no higher (or lower) than a specific price. To reflect the differences in what people in the company would know about demand, pricing, and so forth, each player in our simulation was also given private information that the other players didn't know. For instance, the sales representatives were each told how many chips they would be able to sell to external customers and at what price. Their goal was to maximize their profit margin—the gap between what they had to pay for the chips in the internal market and what they could sell them for to external customers. The plant manager was given information about the plant capacity and the marginal cost of manufacturing chips. The manager's goal was to maximize the difference between the marginal cost and the sales price. All the players were also free to speculate in the internal market by buying chips at a low price in hopes of reselling them later at a higher price.

Even though each player was trying to maximize his or her individual profit, the overall goal for the company was simply to make efficient use of its manufacturing capacity. In this simple simulation, this goal just meant that the company wanted to sell as many chips as possible to the customers willing to pay the most. Additionally, the company did not want to make chips that couldn't be sold for more than the marginal cost of making them.

In the first round of the simulation, our internal market was 86.6 percent efficient from the corporate point of view. That is, the company earned 86.6 percent of what it could have earned if it had allocated its plant capacity and sales perfectly. In later rounds, however, as we tried different scenarios for costs and demands—and as we learned to be better players—our efficiency improved rapidly. By the second round, we were at 95.6 percent efficiency; by the third one, we had reached 99 percent efficiency!

Now, of course, it would be much more complicated for Intel to actually use a system like this. But we have been working with Mary Murphy-Hoye and others at Intel to help make it possible. We are pursuing three primary goals: (1) to design and run much more realistic simulations that reflect more details like uncertain demand, multiple internal factories, and so forth, (2) to refine the software and the rules of the internal market to be as efficient as possible, and (3) to understand the barriers (both business and technical) to actually using a system like this in the future. Driving the effort is Intel's appreciation of the enormous benefits that a market system could potentially provide. Let's look at some of those advantages.

Everybody Can See the Whole Picture

In Intel today, hundreds of people are involved in allocating manufacturing resources. Product line managers compete for factory capacity. Sales representatives lobby to get products for their customers. Strategic planning groups, factory schedulers, and logistics managers try to coordinate everyone else's conflicting plans and desires. But no one sees the whole picture. Even the CEO, who—in theory—is responsible for the whole picture, can't peer deeply enough into the organization to see all the details.

With an internal market, anyone can see all prices for all products in all future time periods. Table 7-1 shows an example (from one of our planning documents) of the kind of information that might be available on the electronic market system. We are currently analyzing various scenarios to see what other information (e.g., all outstanding orders, current factory schedules) would provide the best incentives to people in this system.

Rapid Trading Can Help Companies Adapt to Changes Quickly

In today's world, when something changes suddenly, lots of people usually have to scurry around to adjust. If an earthquake disrupts a critical factory in Taiwan, or if demand for a new kind of memory chip spikes upward, or if the market for consumer PCs dries up, all kinds of plans and schedules must be reconsidered. Urgent meetings are

TABLE 7-1

Hypothetical Prices in an Internal Futures Market for Manufacturing Capacity

Each number indicates the price to buy (bid) or sell (ask) 100 units of a given product at a given location at some specific number of weeks in the future. The columns for Week 0 indicate prices in the spot market for products available immediately.

		PRICE						
		WEEK 0		WEEK 1		WEEK 2...		
Product	Location	Bid	Ask	Bid	Ask	Bid	Ask	...
A	1	2	3	4	5	10	11	...
A	2	5	8	6	7	10	11	...
B	1	10	11	10	11	12	13	...
B	2	10	11	10	11	18	19	...
...	...	...	...	...	...	...	...	...

held, new spreadsheets or slide presentations are passed around, and considerable management time goes into discussions and approvals. Often, companies just can't respond fast enough to avoid a problem or capitalize on an opportunity.

With an internal market, you gain much more flexibility and speed. Individual traders, salespeople, planners, and plant managers can immediately start trading on the basis of new information. In fact, everyone has an incentive to trade as soon as possible to gain an advantage. Instead of having one group of senior managers sequentially working through a single set of options, many people can be simultaneously exploring lots of possibilities.

Let's say that an earthquake disrupts a critical factory. Because the value of factory capacity will immediately shoot up, all the managers of the remaining factories will be highly motivated to reconfigure their own schedules to take over some of the extra work. They may have to postpone other scheduled work, but if the prices in the internal market are more or less accurate, they will know exactly which jobs to do and which to postpone. And all these adjustments can be occurring simultaneously, all over the company, without any single person or group trying to figure them out. The invisible hand of the market coordinates all the separate actions into a single coherent plan.

Internal Prices Can Help Individualize Service

The same kind of process can also accommodate local customizations. Today, if a salesperson feels that accelerating delivery of a particular order is crucial to keeping a key customer happy, he or she usually tries to make this accommodation. The salesperson often has to make many calls, perhaps use a connection with a friend in manufacturing or logistics, and maybe even go up the chain of command to find a manager who will approve the exception.

With an internal market, the salesperson can see immediately how much it would cost to accelerate the order. If he or she has enough money in the trading profit center and thinks it's worth it, the salesperson can unilaterally make the decision to pay the extra cost and (hopefully!) make up for the loss on the order through many more future orders from the satisfied customer. Even if the salesperson has to ask someone else in the organization for help in paying the tab, the exact cost of making this exception is immediately visible to everyone involved.

Internal Traders Can Help Keep the Market Efficient

To keep a market efficient, people need to be allowed to speculate whenever they believe current prices don't accurately reflect actual values. This holds true for internal markets as well as external ones. For instance, if you are a product line manager tempted to exaggerate the likely demand for your products, you have to "put your money where your mouth is" by buying futures contracts for the demand you project. But if others in the market believe your estimate is unrealistic, they can sell you capacity now with the expectation of buying it back more cheaply in the future.

For some people, this role of internal trader—continually scanning the market for potential problems and trading on this information—

might even be a full-time job. It may be more effective, in fact, for people currently in planning groups to exercise their influence as speculators in the market.

Since traders are evaluated on how much profit they make on their transactions, it becomes very easy to see whose actions are effective. People who make a profit on their trades have generally contributed to the company's overall profit; those who don't, haven't. Junior logistics managers in distant field offices, for instance, may be better able to predict actual demand in their regions than the professional planning staff at headquarters. If they use this ability to trade profitably in the internal market, their skill will then be visible to everyone else in the company.

Internal Regulators Can Help Prevent Abuses of the Market

Sometimes, in internal markets, people can do things that are good for themselves but bad for the company as a whole. For example, you might try to buy up all the supply of a given product, create an artificial scarcity, and then charge exorbitant prices to desperate buyers. To help prevent such abuses, a company can use all the powers of the corporate hierarchy (positive and negative) to regulate the internal markets.

For instance, if you think that someone who works for you is abusing the internal market, you can reduce his or her bonus or—in the most egregious cases—fire the person. This kind of market regulation and enforcement will be much easier inside a company than it is in today's external markets. Since all the trades occur on the company's internal system, it will be very easy to spot abuses from the trading data alone. And since everyone works for the same company, no formal legal proceedings will be necessary. Managers can just use their judgment to handle each situation in the way they think is most appropriate.

In the future, some managerial hierarchies may exist primarily to provide the regulatory and judicial framework for internal markets. Management may set well-defined rules about what kinds of trading and information hoarding are appropriate. Managers may also provide enforcement mechanisms for people who violate these rules.

Internal Profits Can Be Linked to Real Compensation

The people participating in the internal market need to be motivated to trade efficiently, but they don't have to be trading with their own personal money. The company might create trading profit centers for each person, and the performance of a person's own profit center might be one important factor—but not the only one—in determining his or her compensation. People might, say, get an end-of-year bonus of 1 percent of the profits (or losses!) in their profit center account.

Some companies might want to weaken these individual trading incentives even further by letting the trading occur with some kind of "funny money" used only for nonmonetary rewards like free dinners or trips to exotic locations. In general, however, the closer the internal market comes to using real money, the better it will allocate resources.

Lessons About Markets

As summarized in the market definition box, markets are based on a communication structure that allows anyone to share information with—and potentially transact with—anyone else in the market. The most distinctive characteristic of a market, however, is this: In a pure market, all decisions are made by mutual agreement of the parties involved, bearing in mind the competing alternatives each party has. As we've seen, markets offer many advantages: They can provide businesses—and individuals—with greater efficiency, flexibility, and motivation.

Does that mean we should use markets everywhere? Of course not. As shown in the market evaluation box, markets have disadvantages, too. By looking at these disadvantages, we can understand better those situations in which markets are desirable and those in which they aren't.

Incentives and Trust

Markets don't work well, economists have found, when the conflicting incentives of participants prevent them from agreeing to things that would be good for the system overall.[18] For example, if you hire an independent contractor to develop a computer program for you, the

---

Markets: Definition

Communication Structure

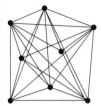

How Are Decisions Made?

Mutual agreement of parties involved (bearing in mind competitive alternatives)

Scope of Decision Making

You must agree to any decision that involves your actions.

Incentives

Maximize your profit: the value of what you get minus the value of what you have to spend to get it.

---

contractor's short-term economic incentive is to get as high a fee as possible for as little work as possible. This may lead the contractor to cut corners in writing the program in ways that you can't see immediately, but that will cause you lots of trouble later on. Fortunately, this particular problem is less likely to occur in internal markets than external ones. If you have one of your long-term employees do the work, he or she will know you're likely to discover any corner-cutting sooner or later. As a result, the employee will have less incentive to cut corners.

A different incentive problem arises when there's a risk that the companies to which you outsource will become your competitors.[19] One of the best-known examples of this problem occurred in the early 1980s, when giant IBM outsourced the development of its personal computer operating system to a tiny software company called Microsoft. Eventually, of course, Microsoft used the strategic leverage this position gave it to eclipse IBM as one of the dominant players in the personal computer industry.

Markets: Evaluation

Strengths

Efficiency

When each player maximizes only his or her own benefits, the resulting overall allocation of resources is usually very efficient (the invisible hand).

Flexibility

- When things change, many minds can work simultaneously on the overall problem of how to adjust.
- Lots of options can be explored simultaneously. Successes can usually be easily seen and copied.
- Anyone can work on any aspect of the problem he or she wants to. The system gives good feedback and incentives that lead people to work where they can be most useful to the system as a whole.
- Even when things aren't changing, the overall framework of pairwise agreements easily accommodates variations in individual cases.

Motivation

Autonomy, motivation, and creativity are usually high because all players must agree to the decisions that directly affect them, and they see direct results of their actions.

Weaknesses

Incentive problems

In some situations, agreements that would be good overall don't happen because they aren't in the self-interests of one or both of the parties involved.

Communication needs

A lot of communication is usually required to find and compare alternatives and to negotiate lots of pair-wise agreements.

A related incentive problem arises with knowledge. If I have a good idea worth millions of dollars, but the only way to make money from my idea is to use your factory, how can we share this knowledge? If I offer to sell it to you, you would be reluctant to pay me millions of dollars until you heard the idea. But if there were no legal way of protecting the idea (such as with a patent or copyright), then once I told you the idea, you could use it without paying me anything. In an open market, the sharing of valuable but unprotected ideas is likely to be very inefficient. But if we both belong to the same company, we can share the idea more freely and the company will reap its economic benefit. Simplifying the sharing of various kinds of valuable knowledge may be one of the most important reasons for large companies to exist in the future.

Communication Needs

Another possible drawback to markets is the large amount of communication they require. Some early economists argued that markets reduce the communication needed to coordinate a system, because in a market, you only need to communicate prices. But that's only part of the story. Whenever markets are dealing with anything other than the completely standardized commodities of classical microeconomics, much more information usually needs to be communicated. If you want to hire a freelance contractor, for instance, you at least need to find out who is available and what they can do. You probably don't want to hire the first person you find, either. Instead, you'd like to compare the fees, backgrounds, and reputations of several contractors. You might even want to negotiate special prices or other arrangements.

All this communicating and negotiating takes time and money. Whether more communication is required in a market or in a hierarchy depends on many details (like what information is needed for which decisions and where the information resides). Often, however, markets require more communication than hierarchies require to solve the same problem. Fortunately—and this is a key point in the book— new technologies are relentlessly lowering the costs and reducing the difficulty of communication. Therefore, while the communication-cost disadvantages of markets may never completely go away, they will matter less and less in many situations.

Standards and "Messy" Situations

One key factor in determining communication costs is whether there are standards for the interactions between different players. For example, some industries (like personal computers) have well-defined standards for how components made by different vendors (e.g., disk drives, chips, keyboards) work together. This means that a company like Dell can assemble its personal computers using standard components purchased from other suppliers. Even though the details vary, many tasks that independent contractors typically do (e.g., graphic design, market research, and software development) also have similarly standardized interfaces.

In contrast, the early stages of designing an innovative new product or starting a new company often involve defining new concepts, new approaches, and new roles—no standards yet exist. Over time, the members of teams in messy situations like these gradually build up a set of shared understandings about what they're doing and how they'll work together. Even these understandings, however, are often unspoken and hard to explain to others. And since the team's understandings are continually changing, it's usually hard to write outside contracts that adequately account for all the possible contingencies.

In general, when a situation is messy in this way, businesses can still use markets to assemble and compensate key team members and to outsource peripheral tasks. But the core team usually needs to stay together as a stable unit until the critical formative phases of the project are complete.

The Choice

Here, then, is the last fundamental way of putting more people at the center of an organization: Don't just delegate power within a hierarchical structure or make decisions by voting; let decisions emerge from the interactions of many buyers and sellers in a market. Sometimes you can do this by outsourcing things you used to do internally. At other times, you can bring the market inside your own company—creating internal markets for products, services, and information.

Both these choices have their own complexities. If you outsource the wrong things, you may find that you have given away your key strategic advantages to your suppliers. If you outsource too little, you may become a prisoner of your own historical capabilities and unable to move fast enough to keep up with your competitors. Similarly, if you bring markets inside your own company, you'll need to develop a new set of infrastructures, a new set of skills in your employees, and a new set of managerial attitudes toward risk and control.

These different kinds of markets, however, are some of the most promising ways of putting people at the center of organizations. And the extensive communication they often need to function effectively is becoming cheaper and better all the time.

CHAPTER EIGHT

When Should You Decentralize?

SOON AFTER LOU GERSTNER became CEO of IBM in 1993, he made what he calls probably the biggest decision of his entire career.[1] At the time, many people in IBM and the business press were convinced that the best course for the "lumbering dinosaur" was to break itself up into smaller companies. By decentralizing in this way, they said, IBM would obtain the benefits of smallness that it sorely needed—things like flexibility, speed, and entrepreneurial motivation. And the market would be able to coordinate the interactions of the resulting companies better than IBM's corporate executives could.

But Gerstner became convinced that the best choice was to do exactly the opposite: keep IBM as a single large company and use its unique size and capabilities to help customers integrate the diverse components of their information technology (IT) systems. In other words, he wanted to use the hierarchical decision-making structures of an integrated IBM to help coordinate all the IT decisions that customers would otherwise have to make on their own (or hire someone else to make for them).

We now know, of course, what happened. Gerstner loosened up IBM's organization but did not break it apart. And his plan worked. IBM's stock price increased by almost a factor of ten during Gerstner's tenure, and many people credit him with pulling off a stunningly successful turnaround against very steep odds.

Of course, we don't know what would have happened if a different CEO had gone ahead with the breakup plan. The spin-off companies might have been even more successful collectively than the integrated IBM was. But we do know that Gerstner's choice to keep the company centralized was extremely successful.

You might think that Gerstner would be a zealous advocate of centralization since it served him so well in this situation. But even within IBM, he advocated substantial decentralization: "Let's decentralize decision making wherever possible, but . . . we must balance decentralized decision making with central strategy and common customer focus."[2] Even more surprising, he believes that the success of centralization at IBM was unusual: "CEOs should not go to [the level of integration IBM did] *unless it is absolutely necessary*" [Gerstner's italics].[3] This level of integration, he believes, is a "bet-the-company proposition." It is often tried, he observes, but almost never succeeds.

You may never face choices about centralizing or decentralizing on the scale Gerstner did, but if you're like most managers, you face such decisions on a smaller scale all the time. How should you make them? How can you tell whether your situation is one for which decentralization makes sense? And if you're going to decentralize, how can you know which kind of decentralization will work best?

As table 8-1 shows, centralized hierarchies and the three basic types of decentralization—loose hierarchies, democracies, and markets—each have strengths and weaknesses. When you need to economize on communication costs or when resolving difficult conflicts of interest is

TABLE 8-1

Relative Advantages and Disadvantages of Different Decision-Making Structures

These comparisons are generalizations only; individual situations may be different.

Decision-Making Structure	Communication Cost*	Individualization and Ability to Use Many Minds Simultaneously	Ability to Resolve Conflicts	Autonomy, Motivation, and Creativity
Centralized Hierarchy	Low	Low	High	Low
Loose Hierarchy	Medium	Medium	Medium	Medium
Democracy	High	Medium	Medium	Medium
Market	High	High	Low	High

*Note: In the Communication Cost column, low costs are desirable, and high costs are undesirable. In all the other columns, "high" is desirable, and "low" is undesirable.

FIGURE 8-1

Factors to Consider in Choosing Whether to Decentralize a Given Decision

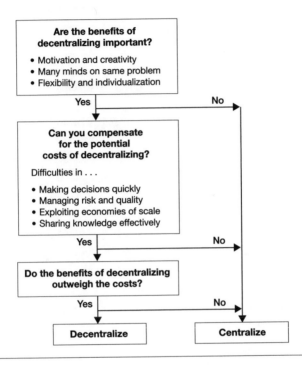

critical, centralized hierarchies may be best. When you need to maximize employee motivation and creativity or tap into many minds simultaneously, markets are especially attractive. When aspects of all four dimensions are important, the two intermediate structures (loose hierarchies and democracies) may work well.

In many cases, however, the best solution is to create a custom system that combines elements of more than one basic structure. You can, for instance, use different structures for different types of decisions. That's what often happens in internal markets: The basic operational decisions are made through the decentralized market, but hierarchical managers choose the participants, set the ground rules, and intervene when the market would otherwise fail to do what is best for the organization overall.

Assigning different decisions to different structures isn't easy; it requires a detailed understanding of your own specific situation and goals. But, as figure 8-1 shows, there is a systematic way to think about the problem.[4] For each major kind of decision your company makes, you can ask yourself the following three questions: (1) Are the potential benefits of decentralizing important? (2) Can you compensate for the potential costs of decentralizing? (3) Do the benefits of decentralizing outweigh the costs? Let's look at each of these questions in turn.

Are the Potential Benefits of Decentralizing Important?

As we saw earlier, decentralization has three general benefits: (1) It encourages motivation and creativity; (2) it allows many minds to work simultaneously on the same problem; and (3) it accommodates flexibility and individualization. The importance of these benefits varies greatly, but they are often especially important in certain industries and business functions. For example, the success of most professional services organizations (such as consulting, software development, and law) hinges on the motivation and creativity of their professionals. Consequently, these organizations are especially good candidates for decentralized decision making. Creativity and innovation are also often particularly important in functions like engineering, sales, product design, and information technology. Here, too, decentralization will often pay off.

But as more work in our economy becomes knowledge work, and as innovation becomes increasingly critical to business success in many industries, the benefits of decentralization are likely to become important in more and more places.[5] In fact, in principle, almost any business activity could benefit from having highly motivated, creative people performing it. Much of the early work in the Total Quality Movement, for example, was about encouraging assembly line workers to look for ways to innovate and improve the routine processes they performed.

So the question of whether the benefits of decentralization are important in your situation is not a purely objective one. It is also a matter of your strategic choices. Different people in the same situation can make different choices about how much they want to rely on the advantages of decentralization. Mrs. Fields Cookies tries to systematize and centrally control almost all the decisions needed to operate its local stores, while Wal-Mart tries to give significant autonomy to its local workers.[6] Either strategy can work well, but you have to pick one and use it consistently.

Can You Compensate for the Potential Costs of Decentralizing?

You may be thinking, "Sure, sure, all this decentralization stuff sounds great in theory, but how often could it actually work? How can you make decisions effectively when no one is really in control? How can you guarantee quality or protect your company against catastrophic losses if no one is watching over things? How can you take advantage of economies of scale or knowledge sharing, if everything is so fragmented?"

These concerns are important—sometimes so important that they'll lead you to reject decentralized structures and stick with rigid hierarchies. Often, though, there are creative ways to deal with the potential downsides (see table 8-2). Let's look at the four main problems with decentralization and the possible solutions.

How Can You Make Decisions Quickly and Efficiently When No One Is in Control?

Sometimes, it just takes a long time to involve everyone in joint decisions and resolve all their conflicting desires. Cheaper and faster communication, through e-mail, for example, helps temper this problem. But even when the transmission of information is free and instantaneous, it still takes time for people to send and comprehend the information. And no matter how much people communicate, they still won't all agree on every question. Each of the decentralized structures offers different ways to make decision making more efficient.

In loose hierarchies, you, as a manager, can sometimes force decisions on people, even when not everyone agrees. In an economic downturn, for instance, you might decide for yourself which groups to cut, instead of waiting for the groups themselves to make such a difficult decision.

If you're a good manager in a loose hierarchy, you probably won't force decisions very often. Sometimes, you'll have to force a decision, such as when a decision is taking too long, when it looks as if there will never be enough agreement, or when people are spending so much

TABLE 8-2

Potential Problems with Decentralized Decision Making and Possible Solutions

	POSSIBLE SOLUTIONS		
Problem	**Loose Hierarchies**	**Democracies**	**Markets**
Making Decisions Quickly and Efficiently	Managers occasionally force decisions.	People vote on some decisions and elect managers to make others.	People buy and sell only when there's mutual agreement, but everyone abides by rules.
Guaranteeing Quality and Protecting Against Catastrophic Loss	Managers control quality of people and results (e.g., with standards) but don't control actions.	Same as for loose hierarchies, except people vote on some decisions and elect managers to make others.	Companies use reputation systems, insurance, performance bonds, collateral.
Taking Advantage of Economies of Scale	Managers occasionally force people to take advantage of economies of scale.	Voting (and elected managers) occasionally forces people to take advantage of economies of scale.	Buyers and sellers discover and exploit economies of scale for themselves. Rules occasionally encourage large-scale activities (e.g., utilities) or restrict them (e.g., monopolies).
Taking Advantage of Knowledge Sharing	Managers provide channels and incentives for wide sharing of knowledge.	Same as for loose hierarchies. Incentives include rewards for sharing knowledge determined by voting.	Rules provide effective ways of protecting, pricing, and selling knowledge.

time arguing they're not doing their other work. But the rest of the time, you should let people work things out for themselves.

In democracies, you can make decisions more efficiently in two ways. You can let the employees elect managers to make decisions on their behalf, as the partners of many law firms and consulting firms do in electing managing partners. Or you can let people vote directly (or via opinion polls) on the most important decisions, as the Mondragon cooperatives sometimes do.

In markets, decisions are often made efficiently because only two parties—a buyer and seller—need to agree for a transaction to occur. If an earthquake disables one of your factories, for instance, and your company has an internal market, then pairs of buyers and sellers can start trading with each other right away to solve the problem. They don't need anyone else to agree about what to do.

But for a market to work well, everyone who participates has to agree on the rules of the game. Markets need legal frameworks to resolve disputes between buyers and sellers, and they need regulatory systems to prevent activities (like pollution, price fixing, misleading accounting, or deceptive advertising) that make the whole market less efficient. In external markets, governments usually provide the rules. But, as we saw with Visa International and eBay, other organizations like trade associations, market makers, or standards bodies can also set rules. In internal markets, the rules are established and enforced by the managers of the company.

How Can You Guarantee Quality or Protect Against Catastrophic Losses if No One Is in Control?

Many people assume that quality assurance and risk management require someone to be in control. But that isn't always true. When the right incentives are in place, just sharing information can be enough to maintain quality and temper risk. Suppose that in your company, the bonuses for everyone who deals with customers depend partly on customer satisfaction ratings. And suppose that everyone in the company can easily call up a page on the company intranet to see the customer satisfaction ratings for each store and salesperson. Just by setting up a system like this, many service-quality problems are likely to take care of themselves without any centralized intervention. Social and other pressures will push people to excel.

Sharing information can work in loose hierarchies, democracies, and markets. But each decentralized decision-making structure also offers other ways to manage risk and quality. If you're a manager in a loose hierarchy, you don't have to watch over or sign off on every action your subordinates take. This freedom allows you to focus on controlling the quality of people and measuring results. For instance, you can devote more attention to whom to hire and promote and how to reward them for the results you want.[7]

In democracies, you can elect managers to watch quality and risk. Or you can let the members of a group vote—taking into account quality and risk, as well as other factors—on whom to hire and promote and how to allocate rewards. Many consulting and law firms, for instance, elect their new partners by a vote of all the existing partners.

In markets, you can control quality in two ways. First, you can use online reputation systems (e.g., those used by eBay, Elance, and Asynchrony) to help people pick high-quality providers in the first place.[8] When online reputation systems become widely used, the traditional signifiers of quality, like brand names, are likely to become less important. Actual user ratings give buyers a much more accurate and efficient way of judging quality than relying on their general knowledge of a brand. Which would you rather buy: (a) a television with a well-known-brand (e.g., Sony), even though previous buyers and objective raters like Consumer Reports rate the set poorly, or (b) an unknown-brand television (e.g., from Joe's No-Name Appliances) that gets wildly enthusiastic ratings from most previous buyers and objective raters?

In addition to reputation systems, the other primary way to manage quality and risk in markets is with various financial instruments: insurance, performance bonds, pools of risk capital, and other kinds of collateral. One of my former students, for instance, used to work in the credit card area of CapitalOne, a large financial services company with a decentralized, entrepreneurial culture. This student really appreciated the freedom that individual analysts had there to make pricing and credit policy decisions for massive mailings of credit card offers. But in 2002, government regulators forced CapitalOne to institute numerous centralized controls and approval processes designed to reduce the risk of huge credit card losses.[9] In my student's view, this involuntary centralization seriously damaged the unique entrepreneurial culture and strengths of the bank.

Could CapitalOne have managed this risk in other—more decentralized—ways? I think so. Here is one possibility: Instead of having a centralized manager sign off on the terms of every mailing, each analyst could have a pool of risk capital. If you were an analyst and wanted to make a mailing in which the total credit offered was below your risk capital limit, you could proceed with no other approvals. And you could still exceed your own limit without centralized approval by assembling a syndicate of peers who together were willing to contribute enough of their own risk capital to cover the mailing. In undertaking a huge risk, you might still have to get approval from a higher-level manager, but you and your peers could manage most of your own risks in a decentralized way.

How Can You Take Advantage of Economies of Scale If Everything Is Decentralized?

Many times, people assume that just because there are economies of scale in one part of a process, the whole process has to be centralized. But you can often get the benefits of both bigness and smallness by centralizing only those decisions involving important economies of scale and decentralizing everything else. In semiconductor manufacturing, for example, there are major economies of scale—Intel now spends about $2.5 billion to build a fabrication plant.[10] But this doesn't necessarily mean that similar economies of scale apply in everything else Intel does. There's no reason, for instance, why the design of semiconductor chips couldn't be much more decentralized. In fact, some of Intel's competitors, like the Taiwan Semiconductor Manufacturing Company (TSMC), take this idea to an extreme by providing only semiconductor-manufacturing services. Its customers, ranging from tiny start-ups to huge multinationals, design their own chips and then pay TSMC to manufacture them.

Even when economies of scale apply, you can sometimes achieve them with very little centralized control if you follow two key practices: share information widely, and provide incentives that encourage scale economies. Many companies assume, for instance, that to achieve economies of scale in purchasing, they need to centralize purchasing decisions. By forcing all the different parts of their company to buy from the same vendors, they get much bigger volume discounts.

But what if, instead of forcing everyone to buy from the same vendors, you just provide incentives for people to form voluntary purchasing groups? If I don't much care, for instance, what kind of personal computer I have, I could just delegate my personal computer purchasing decision to a PC purchasing specialist and automatically get whatever volume discounts that person can negotiate. If I do care, I could look at an online database of the different PC purchasing plans available in my company and decide which one is best for me. In this scenario, the central purchasing people could still have a job organizing voluntary coalitions of buyers, maintaining a database of available purchasing plans, and negotiating volume discounts for the people who choose to participate.

Of course, if the incentives aren't right, this arrangement won't work well. I might, for instance, choose my own favorite PC vendor, even when this is really not the best choice from the company's point of view. But if I am measured and rewarded on the basis of my contributions to corporate profit, then I can balance the potential cost savings for the company with all the other factors that are important to me.

In general, the three decentralized structures allow individuals to make their own decisions about economies of scale. But, in each structure, you sometimes need to restrict individual decisions to encourage economies of scale (e.g., with utilities) or to prevent abuses of power (e.g., with monopolies). In loose hierarchies, the managers do this. In democracies, it's done by elected managers or popular vote. In markets, some kind of regulatory infrastructure does it. For instance, in an internal production-capacity market with only a single factory, the corporation might regulate the factory like a public utility rather than letting its managers charge whatever price the internal market would bear.

How Can You Enjoy the Benefits of Knowledge Sharing Without Centralized Control?

One of the most important advantages of being in a big organization is having ready access to many sources of knowledge. If you're the owner of an isolated hamburger stand in a small town in New Mexico, you have only your own ideas and experience to guide you in running your restaurant. But if you're the manager of a McDonald's in the same town, then—at least theoretically—you have access to the best burger-selling knowledge available anywhere in the world.

Of course, big companies don't always take advantage of their full potential for knowledge sharing. And even when they do, gaining the benefit of knowledge sharing doesn't require centralized control at all. It just requires the widespread sharing of knowledge. When communication is difficult and expensive, the best way to share knowledge may be to have centralized managers find and spread the best ideas from different parts of their organizations. But when communication is cheap and easy, it's often better to have people share knowledge directly through many different channels. For example, independent restaurant managers can share knowledge with each other through trade association meetings, online discussion groups, best-practice databases, and so forth.

In each decision-making structure, you have different ways of encouraging broad knowledge sharing. In loose hierarchies and democracies, one of your most important roles as a manager is often to provide the channels and incentives for sharing knowledge. For instance, when some consulting firms do their annual employee performance evaluations, they take account of individuals' contributions to corporate knowledge bases.

To share knowledge in markets, you need effective ways to buy and sell it. The effective sharing of knowledge is the purpose of intellectual property laws, like patents and copyrights. Some people are surprised to hear that intellectual property laws are meant to help share knowledge. They think, for instance, that if you can't share music for free over the Internet, the laws are decreasing your opportunities for knowledge sharing. But when designed well, legal infrastructures like copyright laws give people much stronger economic incentives to create knowledge and package it for sharing.

Do the Benefits of Decentralizing Outweigh the Costs?

Once you've worked out the benefits and costs, you need to weigh them to decide whether decentralization will pay off. Here, again, however, there are no simple answers—much depends on your particular situation. But some simple rules of thumb can help you think through the choice.

Decentralize when the motivation and creativity of many people is critical. We've already seen examples of this principle in action in AES, consulting firms, internal markets for allocating semiconductor manufacturing, and so on. This principle becomes especially important in certain situations. When your company is growing rapidly, for instance, it is often a good idea to encourage people to creatively explore new possibilities. When your industry is in the midst of rapid change, the best way to figure out how to respond is often to let many highly motivated people try many experiments. And when small groups in your company work independently from other groups (e.g., in a consulting firm or a research university), it's often a good idea to decentralize most decisions to these small groups to spur their innovativeness.

Centralize when resolving conflicts is critical. When the key issue for your organization is not encouraging creativity, but resolving conflicts, then centralizing may be the better choice. For instance, Goran Lindahl, former CEO of highly decentralized ABB, says that you often need to centralize when an organization is shrinking.[11] In times of contraction, hard choices need to be made about where to cut and what to change. Although it's not impossible to make these decisions in a decentralized way, getting people to agree to give up things—including their jobs—is usually much harder than handing down orders from on top. AES, for example, appears to be moving to more centralized decision making now that its whole industry is shrinking.[12]

Centralize when it's critical to have lots of detail—down to a very low level—united by a single vision. Even though sometimes thousands of people are involved in filming and editing a movie, the director usually needs to make many very detailed decisions to be sure that the final film embodies a single artistic vision. Sometimes, this principle applies in decisions about business strategy as well. For example, you could argue that Microsoft's successful strategic shift to embrace the Internet in the mid-1990s was possible because Bill Gates both understood the details of his business and had significant centralized power.

Centralize when only a few people are capable of making good decisions. Sometimes people think decentralization means automatically pushing all decisions lower in an organization, whether or not the people at the bottom have the skills to make the decisions wisely. But such an approach is not decentralization; it's just stupidity. With some decisions, no matter how much information you have, you still need special skills or knowledge to make the right choice. Most hospital patients, for instance, want well-trained physicians to make the key decisions about their medical care, even though the nurses on the floor may have much more detailed patient information.

Similarly, some business decisions benefit from the kind of judgment that comes only from years of experience. Such decisions often need to be centralized. Even in such cases, however, a business may benefit from developing good decision-making capabilities in more people. You might be surprised at what some people can do when given the right opportunities to develop their skills.

Combining Centralized and Decentralized Decision Making

In deciding whether to decentralize one kind of decision, you often need to think about the implications for other decisions. Policy decisions, for instance, can influence operational decisions. Cisco Systems provides an example of how to manage such interrelationships. For travel expense decisions, the company uses an interesting combination of automated policy and employee empowerment.[13] Even low-level employees can make all their own travel arrangements, without needing any approval by managers, as long as they use a designated booking site on the Cisco intranet and charge all their expenses with a special American Express credit card.

Then, when the travel is completed, employees can easily create expense reports online from the credit card charges. If all the expenses are consistent with Cisco's travel policies (such as flights on one of the least-expensive carriers, and cabs and meals within per diem guidelines), the automated system reimburses employees with no management involvement at all. Managers are only involved when there are exceptions.

Cisco uses a similar approach for many other kinds of expenses. As long as the charges fall within automatically administered guidelines, the employees can decide for themselves when and what to buy. More generally, this "automated-empowerment" expense system is an example of how a few carefully chosen central controls can allow more decentralized decision making.

123

In other cases, however, decentralization in one place can interfere with centralization in others.[14] For instance, Cypress Semiconductor gives people great freedom to set their own goals and deadlines (in consultation with their bosses) for various kinds of projects. These goals are then tracked in a database accessible to all employees. In some cases, however, managers appear to use this information, along with their centralized power, to micromanage projects.[15]

Figuring out how to combine decentralization and centralization is still more an art than a science. But it is an art whose practice will become much more important in the coming decades.

Moving from Centralized to Decentralized

Hundreds of books and articles discuss managing organizational change, and much of their advice applies to becoming more decentralized, too: create a vision, establish a sense of urgency, engage people's feelings, proceed in stages, and so forth.[16] This book is not about the immensely complex and important process of making organizational changes. But one question must be addressed, because it lies at the heart of moving from centralized to decentralized decision making: Who decides to make the change in the first place?

In principle, it's possible for a rebellion to occur inside a company—low-level people banding together and seizing power from the centralized managers. But in practice, this almost never happens. Instead, since most of today's organizations are still fairly centralized, the adoption of more decentralized decision making almost always requires the support of very senior managers—usually including the CEO.

In other words, you can't really decentralize an organization unless the centralized decision makers who have power are willing to give up some of it. Lou Gerstner did this to some degree at IBM, as did John Browne at British Petroleum. Senior executives sometimes relinquish power because they see it as a source of business advantage in the long run. Other times, they do it because they are imitating successful competitors. CEOs and other senior executives willing to give up their power, however, are the exception rather than the rule.

Fortunately, decentralization can spread another way—a way that will probably become most common. When companies that are decentralized from the beginning are successful, they grow and take over market share from their centralized competitors. We've already seen this happen with AES, Mondragon, W. L. Gore, Visa International, eBay, and the Internet. In a slightly different way, it occurred in the computer industry in the 1980s. Numerous successful, small companies (like Apple, Lotus, and Microsoft) took market share away from the giants like IBM. From the beginning, most of the new companies were more decentralized than their predecessors. And even though some of them have become much larger today, their internal decision making is probably still more decentralized than that of the IBM of old.

There is also a third—intermediate—way that decentralization can spread: Centralized firms can outsource more of their activities to other (often smaller and more decentralized) firms. This is essentially what happened in the U.S. film industry in the 1950s through the 1970s.[17] Until about 1950, a few large, centralized film studios employed big staffs of actors and production workers, produced almost all the major films, and owned most of the local theaters where the films were shown. Federal antitrust actions forced the studios to divest their theaters. Then, competition from television reduced the audiences for movies. Finally, the recession of the early 1970s created a more difficult economic climate in general. Together, all these shocks led the major studios to shift to the decentralized industry organization we see today. The major studios still play a key role in financing and distributing films, but most movies are made by independent production companies. Most actors and production workers are either independent contractors or are employed by technical specialty firms, and most theater chains are independently owned.

These, then, are the three main ways that decentralization will spread: First, senior executives of centralized firms will voluntarily make their hierarchies looser. Second, decentralized competitors will take market share away from centralized firms. Finally, centralized firms will outsource more of their work to decentralized ones. Even though the transitions to decentralization will be far from easy, they will happen, as managers and entrepreneurs discover and exploit the places in the economy where decentralization is most useful.

The Choice

As communication costs continue their relentless fall, creative forms and combinations of the three decentralized decision-making structures will keep appearing. In many cases, the people who figure out how to capitalize on the new opportunities—whether in big companies or small ones—will gain a significant advantage over those who don't.

The changes won't happen overnight, though, and not every good idea will succeed the first time it's tried. Look at what happened with governments: It took several decades after democracies emerged in the United States and France in the late 1700s for the basic structures to be worked out and begin to spread to other countries. The movement toward decentralization in business began in earnest only in the 1990s, and it was probably set back temporarily by the premature enthusiasm of the dot-com bubble. But the underlying forces of falling communication costs are continuing just as powerfully as ever.

Although centralization will never completely disappear, we are likely to see more and more decentralization in the coming decades. Along with the shift, there will emerge a new way of thinking about the essence of management itself. Traditional command-and-control management won't go away, but a new and very different model will grow in importance.

III

From
Command-and-Control
to
Coordinate-and-Cultivate

CHAPTER NINE

Coordinating Activities

SEVERAL YEARS AGO, when Glen Urban had just begun his term as dean of the MIT Sloan School of Management, Sloan moved up, for the first time, to second place in one of the widely distributed business school rankings. In his remarks at the party celebrating this news, I remember Glen saying that, since he had only become dean a few months earlier, he shouldn't really get credit for the achievement. "But," he said, "I've been told that I might as well take credit for good things like this, because in this job I'll also get blamed for lots of bad things I wasn't responsible for, either!"

Even though Glen did get credit for moving Sloan up to first place in the same rankings a year later, his comment crystallizes one of the most difficult issues for managers in decentralized organizations. How can you manage when you're not really in control? How can you manage when boundaries are so blurred that many people you depend on don't even report to you—and some work in different companies altogether? How can you keep track of what's happening—much less manage it—when the work to be done and the people doing it keep changing? How do you even know what you're responsible for, when more and more people are supposed to be making their own decisions?

No matter how much we talk about new kinds of management, most of us still have in our minds an old management model—that of command-and-control. What we need is a new model. We need to move from command-and-control to what I call *coordinate-and-cultivate*. To coordinate is to organize work so that good things happen, whether you're in control or not. Some kinds of coordination are centralized; others are decentralized. Either way, coordinating focuses on the activities that need to be done and the relationships among them. Cultivation, by contrast, focuses on the people doing the activities: what they want, what they're good at, and how they can help one another. To cultivate is to bring out the best in people through the right combination of controlling and letting go. Sometimes you need to give people top-down commands, but sometimes you just need to help them find and develop their own natural strengths. Good cultivation, therefore, involves finding the right balance between centralized and decentralized control.

Coordinating and cultivating aren't the opposites of commanding and controlling. Rather, they're supersets that encompass commanding and controlling as well as many other management approaches, from the completely centralized to the completely decentralized. By thinking of management in terms of coordinating and cultivating, you open up a whole new range of models, freeing yourself from the old centralized mind-set. And that's what it takes to be an effective manager today—the ability to move flexibly back and forth on the decentralization continuum as the situation demands.

In this chapter, we'll look at what coordination involves. In chapter 10, we'll examine the art of cultivation.

Coordinating Isn't Always Controlling

If you view your role as a manager as controlling an organization, you limit your options: You can set goals that are clear or ambiguous, you can delegate a lot or a little, you can motivate by reward or by punishment, you can monitor behavior or outcomes. Understanding these options (and how to choose between them) has been essential to success in the hierarchical organizations that have dominated most of human history, and these options are still important in many situations. But if you view your role as coordinating rather than just controlling, you suddenly gain a far richer set of options. Many of these options are much better suited to today's increasingly decentralized organizations.

Loosely speaking, coordinating just means organizing work, that is, assembling activities so that desirable outcomes can occur. More specifically, coordination involves establishing three key conditions—capabilities, incentives, and connections—that enable a group of people to produce good results.

Capabilities

People must be capable of doing the things that need to be done. Traditional organizations use centrally managed personnel processes to get the right capabilities in place—through recruiting, promoting, training, and sometimes firing people. In decentralized organizations, capabilities are managed in very different ways. In loose hierarchies and democracies, many people—not just a few—evaluate candidates for recruiting or promotion. In markets and very loose hierarchies (like the Linux organization), there is often no clear boundary between "hired" and "fired." In principle, you can come and go at will. In practice, though, you won't actually do much work unless people trust your capabilities—because of your reputation, your credentials, or some other factor.

Incentives

Good outcomes also require the right incentives. Some incentives are financial—a bigger salary or a fatter profit, for instance. But there are many other kinds of incentives as well: status, recognition, access to information, and the opportunity to do enjoyable and fulfilling work. For incentives to help coordinate a group's actions, they have to be coherent. If everyone has incompatible incentives, even a team of highly capable, highly motivated people won't achieve strong results. The various incentives, therefore, need to be tied to and support overarching goals shared by the entire group.

Connections

The final key to good coordination is good connections between activities and information. Each decision-making structure has its own characteristic kinds of connections. In general, as you move toward more decentralized ways of coordinating, horizontal, peer-to-peer connections become more important and vertical, top-down ones become less important. Here again, shared goals are important—they provide the glue for the organization, bringing diverse activities together into a coherent whole.

The Origin of Goals

Shared goals are, clearly, crucial to an effective organization. In a traditional organization, goals are set at the top by a small senior management group and communicated downward. As a manager of a more decentralized organization, however, you have a choice about how you set the goals that will tie activities together. You can be an orchestrator or a facilitator.[1] If you're an orchestrator, you have your own ideas about what the goals should be, and you try to guide people to adopt them. In a democracy, for instance, you might try to convince key opinion leaders of your views. In an internal market, you might design the pricing mechanisms so that the overall results of the market will be the things you think are good for the organization as a whole.

If you're a facilitator, on the other hand, you don't try to get what you yourself want. You just try to help a group of people figure out for themselves what they want—and how to get it. You might, for example, try to articulate what you think the people in your organization already want and keep testing your vision with them until you get it right. Or you might just provide infrastructures for voting or markets and let people interact with each other directly to determine their common goals.

In practice, there's no sharp distinction between the roles of orchestrator and facilitator. As we'll see in the detailed discussion on cultivation, most managers in decentralized environments combine the two roles in various ways. For example, Jim Schiro, CEO of PricewaterhouseCoopers (PwC), mixed them in managing the merger of Price Waterhouse and Coopers & Lybrand.[2] First, as an orchestrator, he articulated a goal that the combined firm should be globally integrated. Then, as a facilitator, he tested this vision with people throughout the organization. In doing so, he found that many worried that focusing on being globally integrated as a general goal might lead the firm to become slow-moving and bureaucratic. Eventually, as a result of these iterative discussions, the goal of global integration was refined to the ability to be "intelligently integrated at the client interface." In other words, PwC would strive to excel at integrating its resources only when doing so was clearly in the client's best interest. By mixing top-down and democratic goal setting in this way, the firm arrived at a refined goal that was presumably much more compelling for its people.

The Paradox of Standards

Goals help everyone move in the same direction. But they're rarely sufficient—they're often too broad to help people make the necessary connections between their particular activities. One of the best ways to manage these connections in a decentralized organization is to establish standards. If you're like most people, you probably assume that rigid standards stand in opposition to flexibility and decentralization. If you have rigid standards, you can't be adaptable. If everything is standardized, individuals can't make their own decisions. "Surely," you probably think, "the world of decentralization is about getting away from constraining, suffocating standards."

But here is a surprising paradox of decentralized coordination:

Rigid standards in the right parts of a system can enable much more flexibility and decentralization in other parts of the system.

In most real markets, for instance, buyers and sellers interact with each other freely and flexibly because they obey a set of standards. They specify prices in standardized monetary currencies. They have laws (like uniform commercial codes) that specify the rights and responsibilities of each participant. And they have a legal system to adjudicate disputes. If every pair of potential buyers and sellers had to negotiate all these things for themselves each time, the whole system would be cumbersome, expensive, and inflexible.

Standards are much less important in traditional, centralized organizations, because bosses can simply tell people what to do. Two parties don't have to negotiate with each other until they reach agreement; they just follow orders. And it's the boss's job to make sure that the activities each person does fit together to achieve the overall goals.

When people make their own decisions, however, establishing coherent standards becomes critical.[3] On the Internet, for example, rigid technical standards—in the form of the underlying Internet Protocol—enable a tremendous amount of flexibility throughout the system. The "managers" of the Internet act as facilitators by defining the protocols. Then anyone using the Internet can easily interact with anyone else to achieve his or her own goals.

A similar idea underlies the project guidelines of many open-source software projects affiliated with the Apache Software Foundation.

Instead of relying on a single hierarchical manager (like Linus Torvalds for Linux), these projects use a more democratic decision-making method, with participants voting on all important decisions. But each project also has clear, detailed guidelines or constitutions specifying roles, responsibilities, and rules for voting and other kinds of communication.[4] These standards help the democracy work efficiently without the project's having to renegotiate everything every time.

The standards paradox applies inside companies, too. When you have clear standards for the kind of people you hire and promote, for instance, you can often delegate many more decisions to them—as we saw with AES. And when you have clear standards for evaluating people's results, you don't have to spend a lot of time reviewing and second-guessing their decisions.

Bob Herbold, former chief operating officer of Microsoft, says that the standardized financial systems he introduced at Microsoft helped the company become more efficient and flexible.[5] The many different entrepreneurial and individualistic groups within Microsoft could devote their energy and creativity to making and selling new products, not to reinventing their own financial systems. And the company's senior managers could more easily compare the performance of different groups by using a common set of measures.

Standards don't have to be formally written down. Consultants at McKinsey, for example, can easily work together on project teams in all kinds of flexible combinations because they have been socialized to share a common set of assumptions about how engagements are done and who plays what roles. Everyone knows what to assume about what the engagement manager will do, what the junior associates will do, and what a partner in another part of the firm will do if someone from the team calls with a question.

Most of these standards aren't documented in procedure manuals; they're part of the unwritten culture of the organization. But because they exist and are followed, the senior managers of McKinsey can leave most operational decisions to the consultants actually doing the work. The managers still play a key role, however, in maintaining the organizational culture that embodies the standards. In the future, one of the main responsibilities of all senior managers may become defining the rules of the game—the standards—with which the rest of the organization works.

Process Architectures for Interchangeable Organizations

With complex decentralized processes, particularly those spanning many organizations, you often need more than just one or two simple standards to ensure effective coordination. You often need a whole set of interrelated standards. Such a process architecture provides a detailed set of guidelines to ensure that the activities carried out by dispersed, autonomous people merge efficiently to create a unified whole.

A process architecture works like a product architecture.[6] For instance, when IBM defined a product architecture for personal computers in the early 1980s, it became possible for thousands of small hardware and software vendors to work together, with no further need for centralized control. Each company could keep making innovations to its own piece of the puzzle, and as long as the company obeyed the interface rules, its piece would always dovetail neatly with everybody else's.

Process architectures focus on the interfaces between activities rather than physical components. These architectures usually take the form of activity maps that lay out how each activity connects with other steps in the process. For example, VIAG Interkom, a German telecommunications company, launched a new Internet service for consumers in just ten weeks by using a carefully designed process architecture to outsource almost every required activity.[7] One vendor provided the customer service call center, another developed and produced the CD-ROMs needed to install the system on a customer's computer, and still another did fulfillment and logistics. To ensure that all the activities meshed seamlessly, the company's management team worked with the vendors to develop activity maps that documented every part of the overall process. The vendors then used the maps to work directly with each other, without needing nearly as much day-to-day control from the company.

Plug-and-Play Processes

Someday, perhaps soon, process architectures may be shared throughout entire industries, enabling a whole new level of business flexibility. You'll be able to create new processes quickly—and rapidly reconfigure them again and again as your needs change—by using process components interchangeable like plug-and-play product components. Today's most popular term for describing the technological infrastructure for this concept is *Web services*. The benefits of such architectures are so great that, whatever term we end up using to describe them, they're almost certain to become common eventually.

Here's an example: If you're a bank and you want to process mortgage applications, you won't need to write a whole complex software system and train your people to do all the required activities. Instead, you'll use an ever-changing combination of people and software from your own and other companies.[8] You might use one of several automatic services available over the Web to retrieve your customer's credit record. You might have freelance external contractors make calls to verify employment. And you might have a group of employees and prequalified external contractors making the final loan approvals based on criteria you specify.

Li & Fung, the $2 billion Hong Kong–based global trading company, already does this kind of reconfigurable outsourcing with its network of more than three thousand independent manufacturers.[9] When a retailer like The Limited or Gymboree places an order for a certain kind of garment, Li & Fung rapidly assembles a customized supply chain. The trading company combines, say, material suppliers from China and Korea with a factory in Thailand and a group of distributors in the United States and Europe. In part because Li & Fung has developed an excellent standardized infrastructure for coordinating all the activities, the company can fulfill the diverse requirements of its customer base rapidly and flexibly—a critical advantage in the rapidly changing fashion industry.

What will make such arrangements possible on a much wider scale in the future is a set of shared electronic activity maps. Maps will exist for all kinds of processes: making loans, manufacturing clothing, designing Web sites, writing business plans, publishing daily newsletters, maybe even designing cars. The maps will define basic activities (like credit checking, employment verification, and loan approval), along with common variations on those activities, as well as the key interfaces between activities.[10]

A map will typically have many different levels of detail, so that anyone involved in the process, whether working on a major step or a substep, will always know how his or her activity fits into the larger process. And if there's a problem in one step, the person doing it will know exactly who uses the results of that step and will thus be able to consult with that person on the best solution or workaround. Often, the activity definitions will just detail the expected result of each step without prescribing the way the result is produced. The people doing each activity will consequently have great freedom in how they work and will be able to tailor their efforts to the situation at hand.[11]

Also—very important—the electronic maps will include tools for finding people or automated services to perform each of the different activities. For example, there might be a form to request bids from independent contractors to do employment verification, and another form laying out ratings of contractors who have done the work before.

If you're a manager of such a process, your main job won't be to control all the activities and how they fit together. Instead, you'll focus on higher-level objectives:

- Defining the goals of the process
- Attracting capable people (either as employees or contractors)
- Giving them the right incentives
- Providing (or helping them create) the activity maps or other infrastructure they need to manage their own interactions

In a sense, that's how good managers in loose hierarchies have always worked. What's different is that the Internet and other communication technologies make this way of coordinating work possible on a scale never seen before. Indeed, if you use enough plug-and-play processes in a market, you might have a very successful company with no employees at all!

The Deep Structure of Business Processes

The activity maps required to coordinate a complex process architecture are very different from the process maps that companies use today to document their work flows. Traditional process maps are too detailed and rigid. Because they tend to define precisely *how* each step should be done rather than just *what* it should produce, they are inflexible and leave little room for individual ingenuity. What we need now is a means of mapping the key goals and interrelationships of activities at a deeper level—to define the essence of a process in a way that allows a great deal of creativity and customization in how it is actually carried out.

What does it mean to map a process at a deeper level? I like to use an analogy with what linguists call the deep structure of language. For a linguist, a sentence has both a surface structure and a deep structure. The surface structure is the particular sequence of words; the deep structure is the underlying meaning. The same deep structure, or meaning, can often be expressed by various surface structures. For example, the two sentences "John hit the ball" and "The ball was hit by John" have different surface structures but the same deep structure.

In the same way, you can think of a business process as having both a surface structure and a deep structure. The surface structure is the specific sequence of activities that occur in a particular situation. The deep structure is the "meaning" of the process, that is, its underlying goals, its essential activities, and the various constraints on how the activities are combined. (An example of a constraint is that one activity might not be able to proceed until another activity is completed.) The same deep structure for a process can have many surface structures. In other words, there may be many quite different sequences of actions that all achieve the same basic goals and satisfy the same basic constraints.

An example will help explain the concept. Figure 9-1 shows the surface structure of two different—highly simplified—processes for selling cars. Both these processes have the same deep structure: Cars are made by one activity (at a factory) and then flow to another activity, where they are sold (at the dealer). To be precise about it, we can call the relationship between the two activities a *flow dependency:* The "sell cars" activity depends on, and is constrained by, the output of the "make cars" activity. Wherever there's a flow dependency, a means of coordination between the activities is required.

The two surface structures for this process are defined by their different coordination methods. In one—make to order—the cars are made only after an order is received, and then they are shipped directly to the dealer. In the other—make to inventory—the cars are made and stored in inventory until somebody places an order. When the order is received, they are removed from inventory and shipped to the dealer.

FIGURE 9-1

Surface Structure of Two Business Processes with the Same Deep Structure

Activities shown in unshaded boxes are part of the coordination processes for managing the flow dependency.

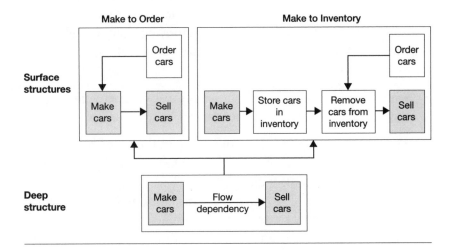

Like the deep structure view, some traditional process-analysis techniques specify the goals of a process and the core activities needed to achieve them. What's different about the deep-structure view is its explicit focus on the dependencies between activities. The dependencies specify where coordination needs to happen and what it needs to achieve, but they leave open the particular method of coordination. The process participants, or managers, choose the best way to coordinate each dependency, gearing it to the situation at hand.

What Are the Key Dependencies to Be Managed?

As the preceding section explained, coordination means managing dependencies between activities.[12] If there is no interdependence between two activities, then there is nothing to coordinate. But whenever you work together with other people on anything, one person's activities will affect the activities of others. You must decide what to do, when to do it, and who will do which parts of it. You must share resources and somehow arrange to have the right things at the right places at the right times. And you must be motivated to work together in the first place.

Managing the complexities of coordination is, in a sense, the heart of management or, even more generally, the essence of organization. For more than ten years, my colleagues and I at MIT, with other researchers around the world, have been studying what we call *coordination theory*.[13] Among other things, we have been seeking the answers to two questions:

- What kinds of dependencies can there be between activities?
- How can different kinds of dependencies be managed?

We have been investigating how theories and findings from fields as diverse as computer science, economics, social psychology, and biology help shed light on these questions.

Some of what we've discovered is encapsulated in figure 9-2, which illustrates a remarkably simple way of defining dependencies.[14] With this approach, there are just three basic kinds of dependencies—flow, sharing, and fit—that can exist between two activities.

Flow dependencies arise whenever one activity produces a resource that is used by another activity. This kind of dependency occurs in almost all processes. For instance, there are flow dependencies from one station on an assembly line to another, from the person who writes a report to the one who reads it, and from the seller of a product to its

FIGURE 9-2

Three Basic Types of Dependencies Among Activities

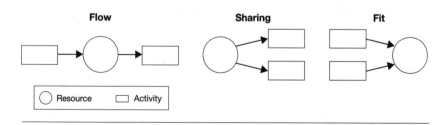

buyer. Most process-mapping techniques (such as flow charts) focus primarily on these flow dependencies.

Sharing dependencies occur whenever multiple activities all use the same resource. For example, this kind of dependency arises when two activities need to be done by the same person, when two activities use the same machine on a factory floor, or when two activities draw on the same budget.

Finally, *fit dependencies* arise when multiple activities jointly produce a single resource. For example, when several different engineers are designing different parts of a car (such as the engine, the transmission, and the body), there is a dependency between their activities—the components they design need to fit together in the completed car.

Our hypothesis is that all other dependencies represent combinations, parts, or special cases of flow, sharing, or fit dependencies. In more than five years of working with these three elementary dependencies, we have yet to find any exceptions to our hypothesis.

How Can You Manage Dependencies?

In managing each type of dependency, you have a choice of coordination methods, both centralized and decentralized. To manage a flow dependency, for example, you need to get the *right thing* to the *right place* at the *right time*. If you're a manager in a highly centralized hierarchy, you (or other people in your management chain) make these decisions. The assembly line is an extreme version of a centralized way of managing flow dependencies: Managers decide exactly when and where handoffs will occur and what will be handed off at each stage. The people doing the work on the assembly line have very little discretion at all.

But if you want to decentralize decisions about flow dependencies, the people making the decisions need to know two things. First, they need to know what the dependencies are in the first place. If I'm a plant manager deciding whether to delay a product batch on the factory floor, it would be helpful for me to know who would be affected by this decision, or at least what, if any, cost would be incurred. People usually know some—but not all—of these dependencies, and making them clear, through activity maps, for instance, can dramatically improve the efficiency and effectiveness of a process.

Second, the people making the decisions need to know what overall goals they are supposed to be working toward. Often, the goals are unclear or inconsistent. For instance, plant managers may be rewarded for maximizing factory utilization, while sales managers are rewarded for maximizing sales. Unless they share a common higher-level goal, it will be very hard for these groups of people to resolve conflicts about scheduling decisions without appealing to a higher-level manager.

Once the dependencies and goals are clear, you can decentralize in a variety of ways. You can delegate more decisions to people in a loose hierarchy. Or you can let people buy and sell things to each other, in either external or internal markets. In the internal market scenario for the semiconductor company described in chapter 7, the salespeople could bid against each other to determine who got the chips for their customers at different times. You might even use democracies to pick the overall goals or the people who will make more detailed flow decisions.

Example: Radical Decentralization in a Consulting Firm

The concepts of deep structure and coordinating dependencies are especially useful in deciding whether to centralize or decentralize a process in the first place. They can help you systematically consider the whole range of possibilities.

Let's say that you're thinking of starting a new management consulting firm and you want to consider some radical, new ideas about how you might organize the firm in a decentralized way. Let's also assume that because you've worked in the consulting field for years, you need no additional research to understand the surface structures typical of consulting firms today.

Your first step is to analyze the deep structure of a consulting firm. You might do this in many ways, each of which may provide different insights. Figure 9-3 shows just one view.

The lines between the projects represent three important sharing dependencies: sharing people, sharing knowledge, and sharing reputation. Within a firm, you draw on a shared pool of people to staff different projects, and this usually gives you more staffing flexibility than

FIGURE 9-3

One View of the Deep Structure of a Consulting Firm

The lines between projects represent three types of dependencies: sharing people, sharing knowledge, and sharing reputation.

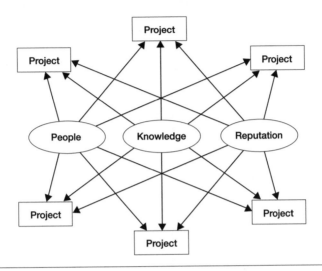

independent consultants have. Perhaps even more important, you can share knowledge across projects within the firm. Sometimes, this knowledge is shared formally with explicit knowledge repositories and practice development projects. More often it is shared informally when, for instance, you call people you know when you have a question. Finally, the different projects within a firm all share (and potentially affect) the firm's reputation. For instance, even the weakest consultants in elite management consulting firms benefit from their firm's overall reputation, and even the best consultants in Arthur Andersen suffered from the damage to their firm's reputation from its auditing activities on the Enron account.

The deep structure diagram shown in figure 9-3 gives you a kind of X-ray view of some of the key problems in managing a consulting firm. But what different surface structures are possible here? To answer that question, let's think about different ways to manage the three key dependencies.

Sharing People

How can you manage the sharing of people between projects? A typical centralized way, used in many consulting firms, is to put people into groups and then let the group managers work out who will staff which projects. But this is only one of many possibilities for managing a shared resource dependency. Table 9-1 lists a number of other possibilities.

TABLE 9-1

Some Ways of Sharing People Among Projects

Each question has several alternate answers, and the answers to different questions can be combined in various ways.

How are people grouped?

- By function (e.g., IT, strategy, HR)
- By geography
- By customer type (e.g., high tech, publishing, manufacturing)
- Arbitrarily (e.g., people are grouped with others whom they like)
- No grouping (i.e., each person acts as an independent contractor—either internal or external)

How does sharing occur?

- No sharing between groups (i.e., you assign people in your own group projects in your own group)
- Temporary sharing (i.e., you can assign people in your group temporarily to other groups when requested by other group's manager)
- Dual organization (i.e., *task managers* staff projects by recruiting people from groups managed by *people managers*)
- Internal markets for people's time (e.g., with computer-based tools for matching people and projects)
- External markets for people's time (e.g., with computer-based tools for matching people and projects)

How are group managers chosen?

- Appointed by higher-level managers
- Elected by group members

What are the incentives for sharing people?

- Hierarchical (e.g., higher-level managers reward you when they think you have shared people in your group effectively with other groups)
- Market (you work on the projects where your skills have the most value, as indicated by how much the projects are willing to pay for you)
- Cultural (e.g., people expect you to help other projects whenever you can)

The table includes some conventional possibilities, like grouping people by function or geography and letting higher-level managers assign them to projects. But it also includes unconventional possibilities like allowing people to group themselves with colleagues they like, to elect their own group managers, and then to "sell" their time to projects using internal markets. Perhaps the most extreme possibility suggested by the table is to have an external market in which each consultant is an independent contractor and project managers use computer-based tools (like those used by Elance and Asynchrony) to assemble teams.

Sharing Knowledge

There are also several possibilities for sharing knowledge among projects (table 9-2). Again, some are conventional and some aren't. In almost all companies, for instance, people routinely ask each other questions, and many companies maintain formal expertise directories to help people find experts. Few, if any, of today's companies, however, rely on markets for knowledge sharing.

Thinking about knowledge sharing in this way opens some interesting possibilities. What if, for instance, instead of starting a conventional consulting firm, you launched a firm that provided the infrastructure for independent consultants to more easily form project teams and share knowledge? The shared knowledge could go beyond the traditional kinds (like templates for proposals and sample results for different kinds of projects). Your shared knowledge repository might also include detailed electronic activity maps to help consultants who had never worked together know what roles to play in a particular type of project.

But if you were an independent consultant, why would you be willing to work with other independent consultants, and why, especially, would you be willing to share your hard-earned knowledge with your competitors? One possible answer is money. By being able to easily assemble teams of people with appropriate skills, you could better compete with large firms without giving up the freedom that attracted you to working independently in the first place. By more easily finding teams that need your skills, you would increase your chances of having as much work as you want. And if other people pay you to use the

TABLE 9-2

Some Ways of Sharing Knowledge Among Projects

What structures are used for sharing knowledge?

- Ad hoc questions to individuals (e.g., by e-mail or phone)
- Broadcast questions to groups (e.g., by e-mail distribution list)
- "Yellow pages" directories of individuals by areas of expertise
- Knowledge repositories of collected knowledge (e.g., previous proposals, project reports, activity maps)

Who maintains the structures?

- Everyone, in the course of doing the work
- Designated individuals appointed by the same groups used for sharing people
- Everyone in officially recognized but informal communities of practice
- Full-time internal staff of knowledge managers ("internal business journalists")
- External company providing knowledge management service

What are your incentives for sharing knowledge?

- Hierarchical: Your contributions affect your performance appraisal and your compensation
- Market: You get paid for making contributions and you have to pay to use the knowledge contributed by others
- Cultural: People expect you to help others whenever you can
- Status: When you make contributions that other people value, your status in the community is increased

knowledge you contribute to a shared repository, you might some-times make more money from selling your knowledge capital than from selling your own time as a consultant!

This sounds good in theory, but how would it work in practice? How, for instance, could you charge people when they use knowledge from the shared repository, and how could you compensate them appropriately for the knowledge they contribute? Here, too, new pro-cesses, with various surface structures, could be set up. You might cre-ate a market in which the buyers pay a unit price for each item of in-formation they use and some of the fee is paid to the creator, or seller, of the knowledge. Or you might charge users a fixed monthly sub-scription fee to access all the knowledge in certain sections of the re-pository. You could then pay the contributors of the knowledge in proportion to the number of times their contributions are used. You might even make all your knowledge and services available to individual consultants in return for a fixed percentage of the income they earn while using your services.

Sharing Reputation

In addition to sharing people and knowledge, consultants in a traditional consulting firm also have the advantage—and risk—of sharing a reputation. For genuinely independent consultants, this sharing dependency doesn't matter much. Their successes and failures have relatively little effect on the reputations of others. But what if you could help a network of independent consultants capture some of the reputational benefits of a big firm?

There are at least two important ways to enhance (and protect) your reputation: providing good products or services in the first place, and then telling the world how good you are (through activities like advertising and public relations). Providing good products or services requires you to do many things well. For example, you must hire good people, acquire high-quality raw materials, and optimize your production processes. One particularly important way of protecting your reputation, however, is by checking and controlling the quality of the final products or services you deliver. Table 9-3 lists some alternative ways of doing this. For instance, a typical form of quality control in a traditional manufacturing organization is to hire internal quality control inspectors to check the final products coming off an assembly line. Similarly, an accounting firm conducting audits will often have extensive processes for managers to review and approve intermediate work products before the final results are released to clients. And, for a typical management consulting firm, an important part of quality control is just the careful selection of the people who will do the work.

To support a network of independent consultants, you would probably want to focus on evaluating the consultants themselves, not all their individual work products. The table suggests some interesting ways you might do this. First, as with many online markets (like eBay and Elance), you can let customers evaluate the work that specific consultants do and then make summaries of these reputational ratings available to other potential customers. This reputation sharing alone will

TABLE 9-3

Some Ways of Checking and Controlling Final Products or Services

When are things checked?

- Before creation of the product or service (e.g., checking proposal or checking people who will do the work)
- During creation of the product or service (e.g., checking intermediate products or the creation process itself)
- After creation of the product or service but before delivery to customer
- After delivery to customer

Who does the checking?

- The people creating the product or service
- Higher-level managers
- Separate internal checkers
- External checkers
- Customers

How are the checkers selected?

- Appointed by higher-level managers
- Elected
- Selected by customers or others who pay for the results of the evaluation

---

go a long way toward giving customers confidence in the consultants they hire. People would be much more comfortable hiring a consultant they didn't know if they knew that the consultant's last twenty customers all told a neutral third party that he or she did excellent work.

It's sometimes hard, however, for potential customers to evaluate previous customers' ratings. For instance, if I have a $1 million project, would I rather hire a consultant who received excellent ratings on twenty small projects of about $100,000 each, or a consultant who received two excellent ratings and one good rating on three previous $1 million projects? And how do I know which customers are just easy graders?

To help potential customers more easily evaluate consultants, you could provide an independent rating service that takes into account lots of information (e.g., customer ratings, interviews with the consultants, and interviews with their customers) to provide authoritative quality and experience ratings. There are several analogies for these kinds of ratings. One is the evaluation of consumer products like cars and television sets from organizations like Consumer Reports or J. D. Powers. Another is the board certifications that medical doctors receive to practice medicine in various specialties.

For management consultants, for example, you could provide overall experience and quality ratings analogous to job titles like associate, engagement manager, partner, and director in a traditional consulting firm. You might also provide separate ratings for expertise in different kinds of projects like corporate strategy, organizational change, and IT system design. That way, a client could choose whether to hire a very senior strategy consultant to do an organizational change project or a more junior consultant with extensive specific experience in organizational change.

But who will choose the raters? One obvious possibility is that you can choose them as part of the infrastructural services you provide to the network of consultants. Another interesting possibility is a democratic approach. Instead of choosing the raters yourself, you might just provide a structure in which the consultants themselves elect the members of their own rating boards. While some consultants might be tempted to vote for easy graders, the long-run interests of all the consultants would be well served by electing raters who were fair and objective judges of actual service quality.

Could This Really Work?

We have just invented a new kind of consulting firm. A community of independent consultants makes extensive use of electronic networks to find clients, to find other team members for large projects, to share all kinds of knowledge, and to share and protect their own reputations. While this network depends on various kinds of infrastructure and services, it requires none of the centralized, hierarchical control associated with a traditional corporation. And yet, at the same time, this new network has the potential to capture many benefits of a large firm.

This example represents a network of legally independent contractors. But if you wanted to, you could use almost all the same ideas inside the bounds of a single, large consulting company. You could have a (weak) hierarchical management structure and pay people a minimal base salary, but most work processes and compensation procedures would resemble those of a network of independent consultants.

Working out all the details and managing the organizational change needed to make something like this new kind of consulting firm really work would be a huge task, of course. It's quite likely, for instance, that you would need to rethink and change many details along the way. But each of the elements can already be found in successful organizations, and something like the novel combination just described could most likely be successful, too.

Systematically Inventing New Ideas for How to Coordinate

You can use the same process to come up with innovative ways to co-ordinate any organization. First, you identify the key dependencies of the deep structure of the organizational situation you face. Then, you think of alternative ways of managing each dependency.

Fortunately, you don't have to generate all the dependencies and alternatives from scratch every time. Many general patterns recur over and over in business. In fact, one reason the concept of deep structure is so powerful is that if you go deep enough, a relatively small number of patterns turn out to be useful in a very large number of situations. If you know some of these general patterns, you'll be able to apply them over and over again without having to think of new alternatives in every situation.

For example, if you look back at the alternatives listed in tables 9-1 through 9-3, you'll see that there's nothing unique to consulting firms. The tables list options for managing three types of dependencies—sharing people, sharing knowledge, and sharing reputations—between projects or products. All the options can be applied to virtually any kind of organization—manufacturers, financial service firms, universities, restaurants, and so forth.

Even more generally, the three basic types of dependencies (flow, sharing, and fit) each provide a set of patterns that recur throughout all businesses. For example, whenever you have a flow dependency, where something is made by one activity and used by another, you can ask yourself, Should we use a pull system (make to order) or a push system (make to stock) to manage this flow?

Even very simple—but basic—questions like this one can sometimes be the basis of powerful new insights. Dell Computer, for instance, transformed the personal computer industry by answering this question in a nontraditional way: Instead of manufacturing computers to stock and then trying to sell them, Dell figured out how it could wait to build a computer until a customer had already ordered it. This pull system gave the company significant advantages in inventory cost, delivery time, the ability to customize, and other areas.[15]

Online Knowledge Bases Can Help You Come Up with Innovative Ideas

There is a second reason you don't have to generate all the ideas about new coordination possibilities from scratch each time: Even if you don't already know the basic patterns that are relevant to your problem, you can look for them in online knowledge bases. My research group at MIT has been working for more than a decade to create a prototype of exactly this kind of knowledge base. We call it the Process Handbook.[16]

The Process Handbook includes a systematically structured library of more than five thousand activities, including basic business activity patterns, important variations, and interesting case examples.[17] (You can see the current version of this knowledge base for free on the Web at ccs.mit.edu/ph.) All the entries are organized according to family trees based on their deep structures. In each case, a deep structure is the "parent" of a family that shares an underlying pattern, and all the different surface structures are the "children."

One of the most productive ways to use our electronic handbook is to find interesting examples and provocative distant analogies for whatever process you're trying to improve. If you were trying to come up with new ideas on how to hire people, you could study stimulating case examples ranging from Marriott's automated system for screening candidates using touch-tone telephones to BMW's simulated assembly line for evaluating potential factory workers.[18] You could also expand your thinking by considering a completely different, but analogous, process: buying. What if, just as people use online auctions to buy things, individuals or companies used online auctions to hire other people? That's not as far-fetched as it might sound. Indeed it's pretty much what Elance and other similar Internet start-ups are already doing!

The Choice

When you view your job as one of coordinating rather than controlling an organization, you can see more clearly your whole range of management choices, from highly centralized to highly decentralized. Sometimes, you may impose goals from the top; other times, you may let them emerge from throughout your organization. Sometimes, you may let people vote on a tough decision; other times, you'll let a market decide on the best course.

No amount of coordination will help you, however, if you don't have people who are ready to work together. In the same way that the idea of coordination helps you see a wider range of possibilities for organizing activities, we'll see in chapter 10 how the idea of cultivation expands your view of what's possible with organizing people.

CHAPTER TEN

Cultivating People

WHEN I GIVE TALKS about new organizations, I often take a little poll to see how well the audience thinks today's companies take advantage of people's abilities. I ask them this question: What percentage of the intelligence and creativity of the people in your own organization do you think your organization actually uses?

Before reading further, pause for a moment and ask yourself the same question. For your employer (or other primary organization), what would your answer be?

The average answer I hear is from 30 percent to 40 percent, with most people being spread out between about 10 percent and 80 percent. A few people might say their organizations use more than 90 percent, and several usually say their organizations are below 10 percent.

Now, all these numbers are somewhat imaginary. We don't really know how to measure the use of intelligence and creativity in a way that provides us with reliable answers. But the results highlight a strong feeling most of us share: Organizations today come nowhere close to realizing and taking advantage of people's true potential.

In the old world of large-scale, mostly routine production, taking maximum advantage of everyone's intelligence and creativity wasn't critical, and the top-down, command-and-control management style was usually quite effective. But as organizations become more decentralized, as knowledge work comes to dominate the economy, and as innovation becomes increasingly important, taking advantage of people's true intelligence and creativity will become one of the most critical capabilities of successful businesses.

A useful metaphor for thinking about the new style of management that this new world will require is *cultivation*. Rather than just telling people what to do, managers will increasingly cultivate their organizations and the people in them. To cultivate something successfully—whether it's your farm, your garden, your child, or your organization—you need to understand and respect its natural tendencies at the same time that you try to shape it in ways you value. More specifically, you try to discover and encourage its positive potential and limit the harm caused by its negative tendencies. Rather than just trying to impose your will on the system, you try to balance the right kinds of control with the right kinds of letting go.

One reason this metaphor is appealing is that it gives you a framework for integrating both the old and the new. As a farmer, my father sometimes took drastic, top-down action: plowing up a field or killing weeds. But every farmer also knows that plants grow at their own pace and in their own way. Even heroic effort won't cause apples to grow from a cotton plant.

When you cultivate an organization, you may also sometimes take drastic, top-down actions, like closing a division or asking an employee to leave. But you also realize that a critical part of your job is to discover and encourage the values, capabilities, and creative ideas already in your organization. No amount of vision and leadership will get your organization to do something it's not capable of doing. What's more, sometimes the most valuable thing you can do is to take advantage of—rather than try to change—qualities about your organization that you don't personally like.

This conflict between centralized and decentralized control—between being in control and being out of control—will increasingly be one of the fundamental tensions of organizational life. Even though people have been writing about decentralized approaches to management for years, the historical forces we saw in part 1 will make resolving this tension increasingly urgent.[1] The idea of cultivation helps you mentally reconcile the inherent conflicts.

The business of making movies provides a prototype of the kind of knowledge- and creativity-intensive work that is likely to characterize many more industries in the future. Kathleen Kennedy, the producer of *ET, Jurassic Park,* and numerous other hits, describes the balance between control and acceptance for a film producer: "Once principal photography begins, the producer steps back and sees where the movie is going. A film is an organic, living, breathing thing. It's not just defined by what's on paper, it continues to change. The creative process continues throughout and out of that comes sometimes the best ideas. But there needs to be someone who maintains a cohesive vision, a focus on the entire picture and not just the individual elements."[2]

In even simpler terms, Roland Joffe, the director of *Killing Fields* and *City of Joy,* talks about the director's paradox of being in control and being out of control: "Being a director is like playing on a multilayered, multidimensional chessboard, except that the chess pieces decide to move themselves."[3]

Managing in this way isn't easy. But thinking of your work as cultivating, not just controlling, helps you get out of the mental boxes of the command-and-control mind-set. It helps you be more flexible and more open to possibilities. A cultivation approach recognizes that sometimes you need to control people carefully, sometimes you need to just nudge them in the right direction, and sometimes you need to accept and encourage the direction they're already moving in—even if it isn't the precise direction you'd prefer.

Principles for Cultivating Organizations

Intuitively, most people understand the dynamic of cultivation quite well. They know that they can control some things, but not everything. They know that people have minds of their own. And they know that sometimes, to get what you want, you have to adapt to what others want.

But the old command-and-control mind-set still exerts a powerful influence on our thinking. It's easy to think that if you aren't in control, then there's something wrong with you. And people often believe that if a problem pops up in their organization, the solution is to centralize control so that it won't happen again. Such reactions, though natural, aren't always wise. Several principles, described on the next pages, will help you cultivate people, not just control them.

Harness People's Natural Tendencies

Any good salesperson, negotiator, or motivator knows that one of the best ways to persuade other people to do what you want is to show them how it will also further their own goals. Dwight Eisenhower once defined leadership as "the art of getting someone else to do something you want done because he wants to do it."[4] In a similar vein, consultative selling is all about how to sell, not by browbeating customers into submission, but by understanding their needs well enough to show how your products can fulfill those needs.

To successfully cultivate organizations, however, you may need to go further. Instead of just harnessing other people's goals to your own, you may also need to adapt your goals to the goals and abilities of the people in your organization. It is, perhaps, no accident that many of our insights about this aspect of cultivation come from the field of politics. Politicians, unlike most business executives, are used to trying to manage in systems that they can't really control. The French politician Alexandre Ledru-Rollin captured an extreme form of this principle: "There go my people. I must find out where they are going so I can lead them."[5]

The need to harness people's natural tendencies is by no means limited to politics, however. When talking about the Linux project, Linus Torvalds speculates that his approach, which worked well for the development of an operating system, might not have worked for a project not regarded as technically challenging by computer programmers: "You need to have a project that many programmers feel is interesting: this does not seem to be the case with a lot of the application programs. A program like a word processor has no 'glamour:' it may be the program that most users would want to see, and most programmers would agree that it's not a simple thing to write, but I also think they find it a bit boring."[6]

The widely used Internet programming language Java was originally developed by one of the best programmers at Sun Microsystems as a programming language for the computer chips in microwave ovens and other household appliances.[7] After seeing little demand for this use of the language, Sun eventually decided to give it away on the Internet. The free language, however, became wildly popular, and Sun reshaped its whole corporate strategy around this unexpectedly important asset. In other words, instead of just redirecting its programmers to other tasks, Sun cultivated the abilities of the programmers and shaped a new business strategy around them.

Let a Thousand Flowers Bloom

Sometimes the best way to cultivate an organization is not to try to decide in advance, or at the top of the organization, which of several alternatives is best. Instead, you can let lots of people try many experiments. Then, when something works well, you encourage it and give it more resources; when it doesn't, you let it die.

Remarkably, the phrase "Let a thousand flowers bloom," used for years to summarize this approach, was first expressed by Mao Tse-tung: "The policy of letting a hundred flowers blossom and a hundred schools of thought contend is the policy for promoting the progress of the arts and the sciences."[8]

As Mao's words suggest, this approach is already common in science, art, and many other fields in which creativity is critical. And as creativity becomes more critical in business, the thousand-flower approach will become an increasingly important part of the new style of management. Some companies already assign several development teams to create a new product. The teams that are most successful in the early stages of development are encouraged; the others are reassigned. Perhaps only one team's product will actually be sold, or perhaps, following the lead of many Japanese companies, several similar products will all be sold, and the market will decide which ones survive.

This approach is also part of the secret of innovation in market economies: Many companies can try out many different ideas at the same time without anyone on top telling them what to do. Many of the ideas may be silly or impossible or useless. There may also be much duplication of effort. But the inefficiency is a small price to pay for the significantly greater innovation.

When it works well, the overall result of this massive experimentation is what economist Joseph Schumpeter called *creative destruction*— a dynamic, ever-evolving process of continuous innovation. Just as biological evolution works partly through an abundance of genetic experiments, seemingly random and out-of-control experimentation can sometimes lead to dramatic economic progress as well.[9]

Encourage Cross-Fertilization

In nature, cross-fertilization can only occur once in each generation of an organism. But because the "genes" of organizations are simply ideas about how to do things, they can be combined and recombined as often as organizational changes can occur. In cultivating innovation and creativity, therefore, one of the most important functions of new-style managers will be to cultivate the cross-fertilization of ideas by creating the right kinds of infrastructures and incentives for information exchange.

In many traditional organizations, information was a scarce commodity. It flowed slowly through dense networks of middle managers, who sometimes hoarded it as a source of power. In new, more decentralized organizations, information flows much more freely. You can use the old communication "technologies" of face-to-face meetings, telephone calls, and memos, but you also have new technologies like e-mail and the Internet. These new methods of communication can greatly lower the costs of exchanging information and of finding the people with the information you need.

A number of large consulting companies now have vast, internal databases of their experiences with different kinds of clients, problems, and projects. Imagine a Chicago-based consultant who wants to approach a Midwestern grocery chain with a proposal to restructure its inventory management process. Tapping into his or her firm's experience database, the consultant can easily find out about previous projects involving inventory restructuring in other industries (including copies of previous proposals, project reports, and slide presentations). The consultant can learn about experiences the firm has had with other clients in the grocery industry and can also find out who else in the firm has contacted this particular client recently. Of course, in theory, the person could find out all these things before the database existed, but because obtaining this knowledge required so many phone calls, meetings, and random encounters, it often didn't happen.

Our knowledge management processes are still rudimentary, however. Few companies have really figured out how to take advantage of the potential for cross-fertilization. One of the key issues is figuring out how to provide the right incentives for people to contribute to and maintain these knowledge bases—to overcome their hoarding instinct.

My MIT colleague Wanda Orlikowski studied one of the first large consulting companies to make extensive use of Lotus Notes, an early system for electronic messaging and collaboration.[10] She found that the consultants made little use of the knowledge management aspects of the system, because they had few incentives to do so. The employees were evaluated at the end of the year on their billable hours, and any time spent learning to use (or contributing to) the system was not billable. At a more subtle level, Orlikowski observed that this organization (like many others) rewarded people for being the expert on something—for knowing things that others did not. Should we be surprised, therefore, that many people were reluctant to spend much effort putting the things they knew into an open database?

One of your key jobs as a manager in a decentralized organization, then, is to encourage this kind of cross-fertilization. And to do this, you can't rely on any single simple technique. You usually need to think about a variety of methods at once: technology, culture, financial incentives, and others.

Improvise

If situations are changing frequently, and lots of people are making decisions, you can't always plan everything from the top down. You need to respond to unexpected problems. You need to take advantage of new opportunities. You need to improvise.

Of course, the more you know, the more you can try to anticipate and plan for all these possibilities in advance. In situations that you already understand well, anticipation and planning may be the best course of action. But in rapidly changing, decentralized environments, you're often better off to just start off in the right direction, with a general goal in mind, and be ready to respond creatively to whatever happens. Many people already take this approach—they just don't realize it (or aren't willing to admit it).

One benefit of thinking about cultivation is that it helps you explicitly take advantage of opportunities to improvise, instead of feeling guilty when you aren't able to plan everything effectively. Orlikowski, for example, talks about three kinds of change: anticipated change, emergent change, and opportunistic change.[11] Anticipated changes are the traditional kind: You decide in advance that you want to change something. Emergent changes are the unexpected things that happen, either good or bad, along the way. Opportunistic changes are the unplanned things you do to take advantage of the unexpected changes along the way.

One organization Orlikowski studied was a $100 million software company she called Zeta. It introduced a new software system to help it track the problems that the customer support department handled from customer calls. Each new problem had to be entered into the system, and all the steps to resolve it also had to be logged. This recording of the problem and solution was the anticipated change, and as expected, it led to better documentation of the cases and more information to help managers adjust workloads and so forth.

Soon, however, other changes began to emerge. The customer support specialists, for instance, began to spend more time looking at each other's case records and developed informal ways of distinguishing reliable from unreliable information. Some of the more experienced specialists became known as reliable sources.

The managers of the department then took advantage of these emergent changes by deciding to make some opportunistic changes. For instance, they reorganized the department to include two tiers of specialists. The more junior specialists took all the new calls and solved as many as they could. Then, they handed off the more difficult calls to the more experienced, senior specialists. The senior specialists also tried to actively help the junior ones on their cases in progress. Eventually, all the people in the department began to be more proactive in contributing their knowledge to the case database rather than just waiting to be asked for help as they had in the past.

The Psychology of Cultivation

It is already fashionable in many business circles to talk about empowerment and democracy, but it would be naive to think that we human animals will ever completely do away with differences in power and control. Most of us grew up in families that had very clear hierarchies, with the parents having much more power than the children. How can all these years of living in hierarchical situations of vast power inequality not have an impact on the kinds of relationships we have in our adult lives?

Moreover, all of us are primates who, as biologists tell us, have biological drives to create certain kinds of dominance hierarchies, or pecking orders. How can this not affect the ways we relate to our fellow primates at work? The answer is not that we should try to do away with all top-down control, but that we should learn to live with the tension—we should learn to balance control and acceptance in the right ways and at the right times. And that is what the metaphor of cultivation can help us do.

Achieving the right balance, though, can be psychologically difficult—even if we readily accept it as necessary. Many psychologists talk about how the interpersonal dynamics in organizations can often be understood in terms of people's playing out at work the emotional dramas from the families in which they grew up. I know a number of middle-aged people, for example, who still seem to be engaging in adolescent rebellion against their bosses or other authority figures in their work environments.

Conversely, we all know control-oriented managers who are apparently satisfying some deep—perhaps unconscious—psychological needs by trying to micromanage everything that goes on in their organizations. And one factor that drives many people to positions of high achievement in organizations is clearly a desire for power over others.

One of my M.B.A. students wrote the following uncharacteristically honest self-reflection in a paper: "I myself would find it difficult to release power in a decentralized organization. One reason is that I personally have not yet had significant decision-making authority even though I would love to have that! Now I am asked to give it up before I have ever enjoyed it."

These conflicts between intellectual understanding and the emotional realities of control can lead to some striking ironies. I have known several highly charismatic executives who were very vocal supporters of decentralization and empowerment—they said all the right words and had many followers for the gospel of empowerment they preached. But if you stood back and looked at what was happening, it was clear that they had created organizations with an incredible amount of centralized power! Everyone focused attention on them, everyone deferred to them, and everyone looked to them for answers. Even though they *talked* about giving power to others, in reality they retained control.

As these examples show, it can be far from easy to cultivate in yourself the right kind of balance between control and letting go. You may think you want to empower people, although you act in ways that put you in control. You may think you want more power and autonomy in your work, but end up seeking out others to defer to. You may think you need to exercise more control in a certain situation, but find that you're not willing to take the required risks. One concept that can help you in these struggles is an understanding of the paradox of power.

The Paradox of Power

In chapter 9, we saw how—paradoxically—rigid standards in one place can promote freedom and flexibility in other places. There's a similar surprising paradox about cultivation:

Sometimes the best way to gain power is to give it away.

If you try to micromanage people too much, they'll resist you, or if they capitulate, they'll lack the motivation to help you achieve your goals. On the other hand, if you give people the power to make their own decisions, they'll be more prone to support you and more likely to donate their energy, creativity, and dedication to your cause. They'll be more successful, and so will you. By giving them more power, in other words, you gain more power, too.

We've seen many examples of this dynamic already. Linus Torvalds gained power by giving it away to other programmers. Dennis Bakke at AES gained power by giving it away to employees. Meg Whitman at eBay gained power by giving it away to customers.

Jim Collins, in his book *Good to Great,* provides a further illustration of the power of letting go.[12] When he analyzed 1,435 *Fortune* 500 companies, he found that only 11 had shifted from merely "good" stock performance to "great" performance and then sustained that great performance for another fifteen years. And every one of those 11 companies had, at the time of the shift, a CEO who was remarkably humble and self-effacing. Isn't that interesting?

Core Capabilities for Distributed Leadership

In addition to changing your attitudes about power, some specific skills can help you cultivate organizations effectively. For several years, my MIT colleagues Deborah Ancona, Wanda Orlikowski, and Peter

Senge and I have been teaching a course about some of these skills. We call it a workshop on *distributed leadership*. Distributed leadership is something you can exercise from anywhere in an organization: the top, the bottom, or anywhere in between. The workshop focuses on helping students develop four core capabilities that we believe are important for distributed leadership: visioning, sense-making, inventing, and relating.[13]

Visioning

In the organizations of the past, you could sometimes go a long way just by being good at doing what your bosses told you to do. But in the decentralized organizations of the future, you won't always be able to depend on your bosses to tell you what to do. Instead, you'll have to figure out for yourself what needs to be done and how to do it. It will increasingly be up to you—not someone above you—to fix problems and seize new opportunities.

And to really cultivate organizations effectively, you'll need to do more than just take the initiative in achieving goals your bosses have already set. Increasingly, you'll need to come up with your own vision of what your organization can do. Unfortunately, the word *vision* has been misused a lot in recent years. In many people's minds, it has come to mean a mission statement full of platitudes. But a good vision is not just a bunch of words that sound nice. It is *a concrete image of some outcome that you are deeply committed to achieving.*

That means a good vision should be important to you, personally. If a vision isn't connected to things you really care about, it's just words. Who else would want to follow your vision if you didn't even care about it yourself? But when you are genuinely committed to a vision that connects with your own deep values, you often have a surprising power to get things done.

In addition to being personally important to you, most visions also require the involvement of other people who have significant freedom themselves. In these cases, a good vision isn't just a way of imposing your own values and desires on others. It also resonates with the needs and values of the other people who will be involved in realizing it. It respects their abilities and their natural tendencies. It helps them achieve their desires, too. In other words, a good vision is not a tool for commanding other people to do what you want, but for cultivating them to do things that they want, too.

Sense-Making

To be effective in cultivating an organization, you need to understand what is going on around you. You need to make sense of what the current reality is—even when it is confusing and ambiguous. In a centralized organization, one of the most important jobs of managers is to take information from many places and figure out what it means and what the organization should do about it. In a decentralized organization, such sense-making is not just the job of a few top managers; almost everyone needs to do it. In fact, being able to make sense of lots of ambiguous data and to recognize trends before others do can be one of the most important elements of your success.

Some people seem to have more natural ability than others to make sense of ambiguous situations. But if you're like most people, you can improve your sense-making ability just by consciously realizing that you need to do so. If you unconsciously assume that things should be clear and that it's someone's fault when they're not, then it will be harder for you to tolerate ambiguity long enough to figure out what's really going on. And if you unconsciously assume that things will stay the same, then it will be harder for you to recognize new trends when they occur.

In 1995, for example, long before most people had realized the significance of the Internet, Bill Gates took time away from his daily responsibilities to focus on making sense of many diverse facts he had received about the new technology. The result was a pivotal memo on the coming "Internet tidal wave."[14] Although others had realized the same things before Gates did, his conclusions led to profound changes in his company. The memo signaled a remarkable turning point in Microsoft's entire product strategy. This, in turn, probably helped catalyze the economy-wide Internet enthusiasm that followed.

Later, thousands of people at all levels of other organizations tried to make sense of what was happening with the Internet. Did the Internet really change everything? Were twenty-five-year-old technologists the best people to head innovative companies and business units? Had the laws of economics somehow been repealed? Or was the "new economy" just a dangerous illusion, and had nothing really changed at all?

The truth, as we now know, was somewhere between these extremes. But all along the way, as the Internet bubble expanded and later burst, many people had to make lots of decisions based on ambiguous data. They had to decide whom to hire, what kinds of products to make, and where to work, using their best guesses about what was going on. Those who guessed well were better able to help their organizations respond effectively to the ever-changing situation.

Inventing

To cultivate successfully, you need more than just a compelling vision and a strong ability to make sense out of uncertain circumstances. You also need to find ways to actually achieve your vision. If the world changes slowly, your vision may well require knowledge and judgment, but it won't necessarily require much creativity. You may not need to come up with brand new visions in the first place, and the old ways of achieving them will usually still work. The few changes that are needed will be rare enough that they can usually be initiated and driven from the top of the organization.

But we're not living in a slowly changing world. In today's world, changes seem more rapid all the time. Today, adaptation to changing technologies, changing competitors, and changing customers is often the difference between success and failure. No one at the top of large organizations can ever know enough to see and understand all the needs and potentials for change. We're living in a world in which lots of people throughout an organization need to be continually inventing new ways to do things. Your ability to continually invent can be critical to your cultivation of people.

As with all the other capabilities of distributed leadership, some people seem naturally better at invention than others. But most people, no matter how creative they think they are to begin with, can enhance their ability to produce creative ideas. According to Don Meichenbaum, just believing that you can be creative can increase your creative output.[15] So can feeling that you are in control of your work and making your own choices.

Many techniques can also help stimulate your creative thinking. These techniques have names like brainstorming, Synectics, and Creative Problem Solving.[16] The word *brainstorming,* for instance, comes from a formal creativity technique developed by Alex Osborne in the

1930s. Brainstorming includes four "rules," which can be paraphrased like this: First, no criticism, evaluation, or judgment is allowed during idea generation. Second, no idea is too "crazy" to mention. Third, the quantity of ideas is more important than quality. And fourth, piggybacking on other people's ideas is encouraged.[17]

Even though the different creativity techniques have lots of differences, many of them have two principles in common: You should separate idea generation from idea evaluation (i.e., defer judgment), and during idea generation, you should try to consider unusual combinations of ideas. And some of the concepts of deep structure from chapter 9 can help you apply these creativity techniques in even more productive ways.[18]

Relating

In the world of business, few important things are done by one person working alone. You usually need to work with other people and other organizational units in some way to achieve your vision. And your ability to manage these relationships is another key determinant of your success in cultivating.

Managing relationships is important to success in almost all organizations, but in decentralized organizations, you usually have to manage more kinds of relationships with more kinds of people in more places. In centralized organizations, your boss—and your boss's bosses—play a key role in evaluating your performance. In fact, if you can just keep your superiors happy, you can sometimes succeed even if many others think you are a complete idiot. In decentralized organizations, on the other hand, you may not even have a real boss at all. And if you do, your relationship with your boss is not nearly as important. Lots of other people's opinions of you usually matter. Your success usually depends critically on how well you relate to many other people at many levels in your own and other organizations.

In general terms, this means you need to consciously invest time in building relationships with two types of people. The first are those to whom you have strong ties—people on whom you depend for resources, whose ongoing help you need, or who use the results of your work. The second are those to whom you have weak ties. These are the people who may have heard news that could be useful to you, whose help you might need sometime in the future, or whose opinions of you affect your reputation and future opportunities.[19]

My colleague Deborah Ancona found that externally focused teams (which she calls X-teams) often outperformed more traditional, internally focused teams, even when the traditional teams had all the qualities we usually think of as good, like strong working relationships and team spirit.[20] What lay behind the success of the X-teams was superior relationship-building. They spent lots of their time on three kinds of external activities: ambassadorial activities (marketing the team to upper management, acquiring resources, and managing the team's reputation), scouting (gathering information from throughout the company and the industry), and task coordination (managing key dependencies with other units).

What Else Do You Need?

Even if you have all four capabilities of visioning, sense-making, inventing, and relating, another skill is often even more critical to your success in decentralized organizations: the ability to manage your own time. In a centralized organization, your boss often "helps" you figure out the most important things to do with your time and "helps" you keep track of whether you're actually doing those things. In a decentralized organization, you're much more on your own. Many talented junior professors in decentralized research universities, for instance, fail because they never learn how to manage their own time effectively in the midst of all the countless distractions and competing objectives and visions.

The Choice

Life in organizations, at least in theory, used to be simple: Managers were in control. They decided what needed to be done, told people what to do, and watched to be sure things were done right. When a problem arose between people or organizational units that they managed, they were responsible for solving it. And the boundaries between companies were very clear.

Increasingly, many of these aspects of the command-and-control world no longer apply, even in theory. Information and control will be diffused more widely in organizations. The boundaries between organizations will often be blurred. And new, information-intensive ways of managing the relationships between people, organizations, and activities will continue to appear.

How can you manage in this new world? Increasingly, your choices will amount to decisions about where you should be on the spectrum of centralization. You will need to move back and forth on this dimension frequently. Some decisions will be centralized, some will be decentralized, and some will keep changing.

To make these choices wisely, you need both hard and soft perspectives for thinking about things. The hard perspective of coordinating helps you imagine and evaluate new ways of managing the interdependencies among people's activities. The soft metaphor of cultivating can help you find new ways to balance the tensions of top-down and bottom-up control. Together, these two perspectives can help you become a more flexible and creative manager as the business world moves from the command-and-control era of the past into the cultivate-and-coordinate era of the future.

But you can't coordinate or cultivate anything without having some sense of the values or goals you are trying to achieve. And that's the topic of chapter 11.

CHAPTER ELEVEN

Putting Human Values
at the Center of Business

In my leadership classes at MIT, I often have my students do an exercise designed to help them figure out what really matters to them. Many other time management and personal mastery programs include a similar exercise.[1] It goes like this:

Go someplace where you can be alone for a while without being interrupted. Take a few minutes to relax and let your daily cares recede from your mind. Close your eyes if you feel like it. Then let your mind begin to imagine something that you know will certainly happen someday—the end of your own life. You may imagine yourself in a hospital bed, knowing you have only a few hours left to live. Or you may imagine your own funeral.

Whatever scene you choose to imagine, try to visualize it as concretely as you can. Who is in the room? What are they wearing? What sounds can you hear? Where are people sitting or standing? What can you smell? What color is the floor? Let yourself imagine the scene for a few minutes.

Then begin to think about what you would like to be true at that time. What would you like the people you care about to say or think of you at the end of your life? What would you like to have accomplished in your life? What would you, yourself, want to know was true about your life even if no on else in the world knew it?

As you think about these things, you may want to open your eyes and make some notes about the things that would matter to you. Many people even find it useful to use this exercise as a prelude to writing a personal mission statement—a description of the most important goals you want to strive for in your life.

If you haven't already done an exercise like this one, I encourage you to do it now, before reading further.

One of the virtues of this exercise is that it helps you quickly connect with whatever is deeply important to you. Not necessarily what your parents wanted for you. Not what your bosses or teachers or friends think you should want. Not what society tells you is important. But what *you* really want.

What many people realize is that they fill their days with details that won't matter much at all to them at the end of their life. And the really important aspects of life are the things they continually put aside, or forget, or postpone. Many people, for instance, say that achievements like wealth and professional success will matter less to them at the end of their lives, and things like family, friends, spiritual pursuits, and making the world better will matter more. Whatever answer you come to, and however it may change in the future, this is the deepest view you have right now of what really matters to you.

Why Do Values Matter?

Why should you care about figuring out what really matters to you? The first reason follows from everything we have seen so far in this book: If you are going to be making more choices in your work, you need to think more carefully about the values you will use in making those choices. Without some sense of what you want, you can't make sensible choices in the first place. And if you don't think carefully about what really matters to you, it's very easy to become confused and distracted by things that don't really matter much.

But that's not the only reason to think about values now. If you want to create a business that truly inspires loyalty and commitment from your employees, customers, and others, you need to appeal to more of their human values than just the economic ones.[2] If you really want to take advantage of a decentralized organization's ability to harness people's deep motivation and creativity, you need to appeal to what truly matters to those people.

And there are signs—especially in the last few decades—that the values we emphasize in business have become increasingly disconnected from the things that really matter to us.[3] For many people in the United States, the tragedy of September 11, 2001, was a shocking reminder that money and material success are not what they care most about. In the aftermath of that wrenching emotional experience, many people found themselves rethinking their priorities, spending more time with family, or giving more attention to religious activities. Of course, as time passes, it's easy to forget what such tragedies make obvious. Life goes back to the way it was. But for many, the feeling of unease is still there, somewhere below the surface.

This, then, is the second meaning of the phrase "putting people at the center of business." It doesn't just mean putting more people at the center of decision making. It also means putting human values at the center of our thinking about business.

What Do People Want from Business?

One thing many people want from business is money. Money lets you buy all kinds of things—things you need and things you just want. Clearly, we want our companies to be efficient producers of economic value.

But people make business choices for other reasons, too. Maybe they've chosen their job because it lets them develop exciting new technologies, feel a sense of accomplishment, spend time outdoors, work with interesting people, travel to exotic places, or spend more time with their family.

Even though the details of what each of us desires vary, our general needs and wants are very similar. Many years ago, psychologist Abraham Maslow observed that all people have some basic needs (like food, water, and safety) that usually need to be satisfied, at some level, just for survival. Once those basic needs are at least minimally satisfied, other things become more important—things like relationships with other people, achievements of various kinds, and finding meaning in life.[4]

In our world today, especially in the advanced industrial regions, many people's basic needs are already satisfied. They will therefore increasingly look to business to satisfy their other needs. And even though money is very good at satisfying basic needs, it isn't always effective at satisfying our needs for things like friendship, recognition, challenge, and purpose.

Ultimately, successful businesses will need to give people a sense of meaning in their lives, which usually comes from making a commitment to some purpose larger than themselves. So, as their more basic needs are satisfied, workers, customers, suppliers, and investors will increasingly look for businesses that give them a sense of some larger purpose beyond just an economic one. Sometimes, this meaning will come from the core products or services the company provides (e.g., curing disease, educating children, or entertaining people). Sometimes, it will come from the way the company makes its products or services (e.g., reducing pollution or providing jobs). And sometimes, it will just come from the decent way people treat their own customers and employees. More and more, businesses will likely compete on their ability to provide meaning.

In a sense, of course, no one should be surprised to hear that money isn't everything and that businesses should think about what motivates people. But many people systematically ignore these obvious truths when they think about business. In fact, many people think that the only truly legitimate goal—perhaps even the only *legal* goal—for a business is to make money. How can we reconcile this point of view with the obvious fact that different people want lots of different things—some economic and some not?

Is the Only Purpose of Business to Make Money?

In the last few decades, especially in the United States, the dominant view of business has become that its only legitimate goal is to make money for its stockholders. As recently as 1981, for instance, the Business Roundtable (a group of chief executives of the two hundred largest U.S. companies) declared that one job of managers was to balance the legitimate claims of all the constituencies of a business: shareholders, customers, employees, communities, suppliers, and society at large. But by 1997, the same group was saying the opposite in its Statement on Corporate Governance: "The notion that the board must somehow balance the interests of stockholders against the interests of other stakeholders fundamentally misconstrues the role of directors." The paramount duty of managers and directors was only to stockholders, the executives said, not to any other stakeholders.[5]

Perhaps the most articulate and influential statement of this view appears in a famous 1970 *New York Times Magazine* article by Milton Friedman. Friedman says that the *only* social responsibility of a business is to "engage in activities designed to increase its profits so long as it stays within the rules of the game."[6] His basic argument was that the individual stockholders, employees, and customers of a company should be able to decide for themselves what social or other causes they want to support with their money; the corporation shouldn't make those decisions for them.

Of course, Friedman would say that you shouldn't do anything in business that is illegal or unethical. And sometimes, good deeds help you make more money. For instance, treating your employees well may help you attract talent, just as donating to local charities may get you more favorable treatment from local governments. Advertising that your products are environmentally friendly may also help you sell more of them. But according to this view, you should never do good things like these unless they have a reasonable prospect of helping your business financially in the long run. Doing them just because they're the right thing to do is never reason enough.

There is an appealing logic to this argument, which provides a refreshing clarity in our thinking about a fuzzy topic. In many cases, profit is a very good measure of how well you are doing, whatever it is you are supposed to be doing. But unfortunately, the logic doesn't apply nearly as widely as many people think it does.[7]

Friedman's whole argument is based on the premise that the managers of a business work for the owners of the business. In large, publicly held companies, he says, the desires of the owners "*generally* will be to make as much money as possible while conforming to the basic rules of society" [my italics]. Friedman explicitly makes exceptions for businesses owned by individual proprietors and by groups of people who establish corporations for other purposes (such as to run hospitals or schools).

But those are huge loopholes! Friedman certainly doesn't say that businesses should only do things that are in their financial interest. He only says that businesses should serve the desires of their owners, whatever those desires are.

But who are the owners of businesses, and what do they want? Why, they are people, of course! And people have many desires, some financial and some not. Why shouldn't people take into account their non-financial values in deciding how to invest their money, just as they take them into account in other parts of their lives?

One simple example of this is the growth of so-called socially responsible investment funds. These funds screen their investments to eliminate companies that engage in practices the fund managers (and their investors) consider socially undesirable. Conversely, the funds include companies engaged in socially desirable activities.

Of course, not everyone agrees on what is socially desirable, and different fund managers are free to define their criteria however they want. Common criteria eliminate companies that profit from gambling and the sale of products like tobacco, weapons, and alcohol, but different funds can use opposite criteria on controversial issues like birth control and abortion.[8]

Many people think of socially responsible investing as a liberal cause, concerned mostly with saving the environment, protecting workers' rights, and so forth. But there are also very conservative funds that make "biblically based pro-life, pro-family" investments.[9] In principle, there's no reason that any political, religious, or other interest group— from the far right to the far left—couldn't create its own fund.

At first, these socially responsible funds were a very small niche in the investment world, but since the 1990s, they have become mainstream. According to a 2001 report, almost 12 percent of all funds under professional management in the United States use socially responsible investing in some way.[10]

As these socially responsible funds demonstrate, you can select companies you want to invest in based on whether the business activities they conduct correspond to your values. But can a large, publicly held corporation legitimately pursue a nonfinancial goal as its primary objective? The answer is yes. Johnson & Johnson, for instance, takes very seriously its credo that explicitly puts the interests of its customers, employees, and communities ahead of its stockholders. For instance, when its Tylenol was implicated in the deaths of seven people in 1982, the company rapidly removed the product from store shelves all over the United States. It didn't start selling the product again until it had developed a tamper-proof container. Today, we think of Johnson & Johnson's actions as a great example of good public relations. In fact, Johnson & Johnson's example has set the standard for other companies in the years since. But at the time, the company's action was extremely risky for its reputation and finances.

We've already seen another example of a large, public company that explicitly puts nonfinancial goals ahead of financial ones. As AES cofounder Dennis Bakke says, "We never set out to be the most efficient or most powerful or richest company in the world—only the most fun."[11] There is nothing in Friedman's argument that says companies can't or shouldn't pursue nonfinancial goals, as long as their investors agree.

How Can a Group of People Decide What Values to Pursue?

But if it's OK to have nonfinancial goals in a business, where do you draw the line? Who gets to choose what goals to have? Investors aren't the only people whose agreement is needed for a company to be successful. If a company is to be successful, all the other stakeholders, including employees, customers, and suppliers, also have to voluntarily chose to do business with it. Even the society at large has to "agree" to let a company exist and do business.[12]

All these stakeholders often have different views about what a company's goals should be. So, who gets to decide? The decision, in the end, is like any other business decision. Any of the decision-making structures described in part 2 could be used to make it. One of the most intriguing possibilities is to use the most decentralized structure of all—markets. You might call this a marketplace for values.

A Marketplace for Values

In a marketplace for values, decisions about values would be made—as they are in any marketplace—by mutual agreements between the people directly involved. You can try to pursue whatever values are important to you (and not illegal), but you will only succeed if you find other people who agree with your values. Those who share your values—and who believe you are doing a good job of pursuing them—will be more likely to work for you, hire you, buy your products, or invest in your company.

In fact, we already have such a marketplace for values. We live in it, though we don't usually think about it in this way. Consumers, for instance, can decide to buy from companies whose values they like and refuse to buy from companies whose values they don't like. Some people, for example, choose to buy what they consider wholesome family movies from Disney. Other people boycott Disney products because they believe Disney creates antifamily entertainment and supports nonmarried lifestyles.[13]

Companies can consciously choose to appeal to these different kinds of values. British Petroleum, for example, has made major changes in its corporate strategy and advertising to focus on new, environmentally friendly energy sources that are "beyond petroleum."[14]

Employees also express their values in choosing where to work. When Nike was receiving bad press for the labor practices of its contractors, the morale of its own employees fell. According to Maria Eitel, Nike's vice president for corporate social responsibility, "[the employees] were going to barbecues and people would say: 'How can you work for Nike?' I don't know if we were losing employees but it sure . . . didn't help in attracting them."[15]

On the other hand, when a particular set of values becomes popular, it becomes much easier for organizations that represent those values to recruit employees. The Central Intelligence Agency, for instance, received more than three times as many job applications in the nine months after the terrorist attacks of September 11, 2001, than in the same period a year earlier.[16]

As these examples show, people's noneconomic values already play a major role in their economic decisions. Of course, markets also impose some economic constraints on their value decisions. For instance, people can't work indefinitely in a business that appeals to their values unless the business is also making a profit or has some other source of money. And markets are not ideal for making all value decisions. For example, people with more money generally have more influence in market decisions than people with less money. But unequal decision-making power is not unique to markets. In democratic decision making, opinion leaders and people who control the mass media have much more influence than do ordinary voters.

In spite of their limitations, markets have some appealing properties for making decisions about values: As an individual, you can express your values directly in choosing what to buy, where to work, how to do your job, and where to invest. Companies can compete for customers, employees, and investors not just on the basis of the products they make, but also on the basis of the values they represent. Everyone gets to choose the people and companies to interact with, and no one is bound by a decision to which he or she didn't agree. The result of all these mutual agreements is that the market continually shifts resources in ways that are consistent with the values of the people participating. To paraphrase a cliché, people in a marketplace for values—like people in a democracy—get the society they deserve.

Will a marketplace for values always result in outcomes you like personally? No. Will it always result in things that other people would consider socially responsible? No. Are there times when we need to put democratically chosen constraints on this process? Absolutely. But perhaps—if we use it consciously and appropriately—the flexible, decentralized process of marketplace decision making is a far better way of achieving many noneconomic goals than we usually realize.

Transparency

As more businesses try to pursue noneconomic goals, one of the most obvious dangers is that some people will cynically try to exploit others' good intentions. For example, if lots of people want to work for companies that are socially responsible, some businesses will try to do highly visible, politically popular things to appear socially responsible, even when daily life inside these companies is far from desirable.

Before its notorious accounting and other scandals, Enron Corporation had a widely distributed sixty-four-page code of ethics about the "moral and honest manner" in which the company's business should be conducted.[17] And some of the most visible examples of "socially responsible" businesses (like The Body Shop) have been heavily criticized for the sometimes conflicting reality behind the images they promote.[18]

Of course, it's not easy to judge any of these cases from the outside. But the world of business has always included people who are good at cynically manipulating others to achieve their own ends. And if people's desires for noneconomic values increase, these cynical manipulators will just have a stronger economic incentive to exploit people in new ways.

For this process to work well, therefore, it needs something else. It needs to be transparent. People need to make their choices about values based on accurate information. Now, *transparent* is just another way of saying that lots of accurate information is communicated to lots of people. And, fortunately, new communication technologies are making this kind of transparency cheaper and easier than ever before.

Today, most of our value-based choices as consumers rely on extremely limited information. Your knowledge about Nike, for example, comes from a combination of consumer activists, investigative journalists, and Nike's own public relations team. None of these groups is unbiased. And even if you have some (possibly biased) information about Nike, you don't know how Nike's practices compare with those of its competitors.

Wouldn't it be nice if there were a systematic, unbiased way of finding out how different companies perform on various measures of values that are important to you? In other words, what if there were the equivalent of accountants and auditors for nonfinancial measures as well as financial ones?

In fact, such steps are already being taken. Many companies are beginning to measure themselves on a so-called triple bottom line: financial, social, and environmental (or "profits, people, and planet"). Dozens of companies all over the world, from ABB in Switzerland to Yasuda Fire and Marine Insurance in Japan, are making detailed public reports on quantitative measures of things like their greenhouse gas emissions, recycling, and workplace injuries.[19] As this kind of information becomes standardized and widely available, people will be able to use it in making their own decisions about where to invest, where to work, and where to buy.

IdealsWork

One of the most intriguing efforts in using new technologies to increase transparency is a Web site called IdealsWork (www.idealswork. com). This site helps consumers compare the social and environmental performance of thousands of product brands according to the user's own individual values. From various categories, such as the environment, women's issues, minority issues, labor practices, animal rights, weapons, and nuclear energy, you select whatever values are important to you. Most of the values included so far are politically liberal concerns, but there's no reason, in principle, why sites like this couldn't include issues of interest to political conservatives or Catholics or Buddhists or gun owners or any other interest group.

Once you've selected a set of values, you can see rankings of different brands in a specified product category. The ratings are based, according to the site, on "objective, 'hard' data—such as the number of tons of toxic waste a company has released into the atmosphere, or the number of women on its Board of Directors," for a precise time window, called a reporting period.[20]

For example, when I compared brands of recreational footwear on the dimensions of labor issues and human rights, Nike, surprisingly, fell nowhere near the bottom.[21] Instead, the company was near the middle of the list. Brands like Dr. Scholl's, Stride Rite, and Keds rated more highly, and others like Reebok, Rockport, and FootJoy rated worse. By making these kinds of value-based comparisons far easier and more accurate than ever before, Web sites like this one make it much more likely that people can take whatever noneconomic values matter to them into account in making their buying decisions.

The Choice

So far in this book, we've learned about the changes that information technology is enabling in the ways that work is organized. We've learned about what these new possibilities will look like and what they mean for you as a manager. And we've learned about how, in order to take advantage of these changes in business, you need to understand the whole range of human values—not just the narrowly economic ones—that will drive these changes.

But what do these changes mean for you as a person? What do they mean for the things that matter most deeply to you?

For one thing, you'll probably have more freedom to pursue whatever you care most about. Maybe, for you, it's simply a desire to spend more time on the important things in life like families and friends. Maybe it's about providing financial support to the people you love.

Or maybe you are trying to make the world a better place in a social, political, or technological sense.

Whatever is important to you, you probably have more opportunity than you may realize to pursue those things in business, even in for-profit companies. You don't have to be limited by the misconception that corporations always have to try to maximize their profits. Nor must you be limited by what other people think are the social responsibilities of business. You are really only limited by what you can imagine and by what you can find other people to support.

And, to a degree that few people have realized, new communication technologies like the Internet make it more feasible to do this than ever before. By greatly easing the sharing of information, they make it easier for you to find other people and companies that share your values. They also make it easier to discover what other people and companies actually do and how their behavior corresponds with their values. Thus, communication technologies can help us make markets much more transparent and much more efficient—not just at achieving economic goals, but also at achieving noneconomic ones.

Cultivating Your Values

No matter how strongly you want something and how hard you work toward it, you may not get it. Just as it's not always easy to make money, it's not always easy to achieve noneconomic goals. We live in an incredibly complex, decentralized world that none of us completely controls. Sometimes, even little things you do can have huge effects. Other times, no matter how hard you try, all your efforts seem wasted.

But even though you can't completely control your world, you can cultivate it according to your own values. Idries Shah, the modern Sufi teacher, describes this process:

> [Man] "finds himself," if he would only accept it, not in any static world or society, but in environments which only *look* like this. He does not live very long, he can control very little of his circumstances, and the things which happen to him, even in the most highly structured environments, may have far more effect on his life than the things which he causes to happen: however

much he may strive, and irrespective of whether or not he believes the reverse to be true.

. . . So you could say that the Sufi dominates his environment by being able when necessary, to stand aside from it, allowing it to have only the minimum effect on him, and by meshing with it, when indicated; while the individual (especially in the West) very often tries to dominate it by thrusting all his weight against it, marshalling every form of energy he can think of. The one attitude has largely produced the Western world, the other, much of the Eastern. But in mutual usefulness they are not as far apart as one might imagine.[22]

If you are trying to control a system, you apply all your effort to making the outcomes of the system be what you want. If, on the other hand, you are trying to cultivate a system, you are not attached to the outcomes in the same way. For example, if you identify too strongly with your children's successes and failures, you may prevent them from fulfilling their own true potential. In contrast, when you cultivate your children's development, you try to understand their natural possibilities and to encourage in them the things you value. But you know that bad outcomes will sometimes result, no matter what you do, and good outcomes may happen in spite of you.

Similarly, in business, if you try too hard to accomplish particular goals you think are good, you may fail to see even better things that are emerging. And, no matter how hard you try, many other factors besides your own efforts will determine the outcomes.

How Can You Know What to Do?

How can you possibly know what to do in the midst of all this complexity? The answer that almost all the world's major religious and spiritual teachers have suggested in some form is to listen to your own inner voice.[23] Ultimately, this perspective—more than any logical analysis or political argument—is your most reliable guide to what is really good in a given situation.

But for your inner voice to be a reliable guide, you have to learn to hear it. If your mind is too full of greed, ambition, or pride in your own goodness, you won't be able to perceive what is actually good.

Moving beyond these obstacles has always been one of the most important goals of personal and spiritual development.

I can think of no better way to summarize this idea than with this passage from the conclusion of E. F. Schumacher's classic book *Small Is Beautiful*:

> Everywhere people ask: "What can I actually *do?*" The answer is as simple as it is disconcerting: we can, each of us, work to put our own inner house in order. The guidance we need for this work cannot be found in science or technology, the value of which utterly depends on the ends they serve; but it can still be found in the traditional wisdom of mankind.[24]

Epilogue

WE HUMANS have come a long way from our earliest hunter-gatherer bands to the increasingly networked, decentralized organizations of today. At each step along the way, new technologies like writing, the printing press, and now the Internet were key enablers of our progress. While centralized hierarchies are in no danger of going away, new technologies are now making it feasible—on a scale never before possible—to make more and more business decisions in more decentralized ways, through loose hierarchies, democracies, and markets. Managing successfully in this world will require you to expand your managerial repertoire beyond the traditional model of command and control to a broad range of ways to coordinate and cultivate—both centralized and decentralized.

All along the way, the key drivers of our progress have been our own human values—our desires for material well-being, for freedom, and for all the other things that matter to us. Whether we think consciously about them or not, our values influence the choices we make. And if we want to make those choices wisely, we need to think deeply about the things that really matter to us. Either way, the choices we make now about how to use the amazing potential of information technology to organize work will shape our future for many decades to come.

As I write this epilogue in the spring of 2003, there are plenty of signs of trouble in the world. In the last few years, many stock price indexes have lost more value than at any time since the Great Depression, and the prospects for economic recovery are still very uncertain. Fighting continues in the Middle East, and we face the very real possibility of an expanding worldwide war of terrorism, perhaps even a global confrontation across cultural and religious lines.

In troubled times like these, we humans are often tempted to retreat. We look to powerful centralized leaders to save and protect us.

We want to go back to the way things used to be. We want to stop worrying about "luxuries" like social values. And we want to stop experimenting with new ways of doing things.

Tempting as it may be, however, a retreat may be exactly the wrong way out of our present problems. Perhaps the solution to our problems lies not in going back to the old ways, but in going forward to the new ones; not in looking to authority figures to protect us, but in figuring out for ourselves new things to try; not in focusing ever more closely on the economic bottom line, but in looking deep within ourselves for the things that really matter.

Of course, there are no easy answers here. Figuring out for yourself how to do your work and live your life in ways consistent with your own deepest values is no easier now than it ever was. But one of the most important messages in this book is that you probably have more choices than you realize in your work and your life. And in this time of vast change in the world, your choices probably have more impact than you realize in shaping our world for the rest of this century.

By the time you read these words, the problems I see around me today may have become much worse, or they may have gone away. In the short term, you may see signs of increasing centralization, or you may see the opposite.

But regardless of the short-term ups and downs always present in human affairs, the deep forces we've seen in this book will continue to work their way through our businesses and our societies, year after year and decade after decade.

Where will it all end?

Of course, we don't know for sure. But when future generations look back at the history of business, they will likely realize that the huge, centralized, hierarchical corporations of the twentieth century were not the pinnacle of business organization. Instead, they may see these "traditional" corporations as merely a temporary aberration—an interlude of centralization—between periods of largely decentralized organizations.

But the decentralized organizations of the twenty-first century, unlike their predecessors, will be able to take advantage of the benefits of both bigness and smallness. They'll give individuals lots of flexibility and freedom, but they'll also integrate people and activities all over the world on a scale never before even remotely possible in the history of humanity. The powerful economic and technological forces pushing in this direction make this outcome very likely indeed.

But one aspect of the future is less certain: Will this be a world that is not only more efficient economically, but also better for the people who live in it?

That is up to you.

How Do Communication Costs Affect Centralization?

A Simple Model

AS THIS BOOK HAS SHOWN, communication costs can play a pivotal role in determining how decision-making power is distributed in organizations. A simple model can help reveal why this is so—and provide guidance in choosing whether to centralize or decentralize.[1]

The model highlights the role of two critical factors: (1) the cost of communication and (2) the value of remote information. The cost of communication itself has two parts: the *unit cost* of communicating a "unit" of information over a fixed distance, and the *total cost* of all communications required for a given decision. If, for example, you're trying to choose a new supplier, you might fax one of the candidate companies a list of specifications. The unit cost of sending the fax through the telephone system might be fifty cents. The total cost of communication for deciding which supplier to use would, however, encompass all the costs of all the letters mailed, proposals exchanged, meetings held, and telephone calls made between you and all the potential suppliers. In general, as information technologies improve, the unit costs of communication decrease. The total costs, however, may go up, go down, or remain unchanged, depending on how changes in the unit costs affect the demand for communication.

The second factor, the value of remote information, can also be divided into two parts: the *potential value* and the *actual benefit*. The potential value is how much information from other places would be worth to you if you actually used it. In some cases, like deciding how to respond to an angry customer in your store, most of the information you need to make your decision is right in front of you: what the customer is saying, the look on his or her face, and the facts about what caused him or her to be upset. For this decision, therefore, the potential value of information from other places is low. But in other cases—deciding what kinds of products to order for the fall season, say—the potential value of remote information about prices, market trends, delivery times, and so on, may be very high.

The actual benefit of remote information hinges on whether you used the information in making your decision. If you didn't use the information, then its actual benefit to you was zero; if you did use it, then the model assumes that you realized its full potential value. (Sometimes, of course, information provides less actual benefit to you than your estimate of its potential. In this simple model, however, we don't worry about this subtlety. We just define the potential value as the benefit you would actually receive if you used the information.) In general, the potential value of remote information for a particular decision does not change as communication costs change. As communication costs decrease, however, your actual benefits usually increase, because you can afford to use more of the information that was always potentially available.

Many other factors also influence choices about centralization and decentralization.[2] For the purposes of this model, these are lumped into a catch-all category called "all other costs." This category can include things like whether you trust remote decision makers to make good decisions, whether remote decision makers are more motivated when they feel they are making their own decisions, the salaries for decision makers, the economies of scale (or the lack thereof), and many other factors. In general, these factors don't change as communication costs change, but they can have a very important effect on whether centralization (or decentralization) is desirable in the first place and on the effects of changing communication costs.

How Do These Factors Work Together for Different Kinds of Decisions and Different Decision-Making Structures?

Remember the three decision-making structures we have seen throughout the history of societies and businesses: independent, centralized,

FIGURE A-1

Three Basic Decision-Making Structures Used in Societies and Businesses

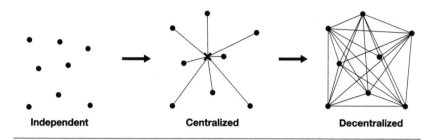

| Independent | Centralized | Decentralized |

and decentralized decision making. These structures are shown again in figure A-1.

Table A-1 summarizes the relative costs and benefits of these three decision-making structures. As the table shows, independent decision makers have the lowest total costs of communication (because, by definition, they do the least communicating). Next come centralized decision makers, followed by decentralized decision makers. Furthermore, both centralized and decentralized decision makers realize the actual benefit of remote information that independent decision makers don't use.

The costs of all the other factors for the different decision-making structures are more situation-dependent. Therefore, I just represent them by question marks in the table.

TABLE A-1

Summary of Costs and Benefits for Various Decision-Making Structures

Decision-Making Structure	Total Costs of Communication	Actual Benefits of Remote Information	All Other Costs (Trust, Motivation, etc.)
Independent	Low	Low	?
Centralized	Medium	High	?
Decentralized	High	High	?

How do these different kinds of costs trade off against each other in different situations? To answer this question, we need to consider the potential value of remote information for a given decision, and the unit costs of communicating the information. Figure A-2 shows the relationship between these two factors. For each point on the graph, the figure also shows which decision-making structure would be most desirable.

Of course, the exact locations of the regions for which different decision-making structures are desirable depend on the exact costs and benefits in the structures. Remarkably, however, the shapes and relative positions of the regions in figure A-2 follow mathematically from just the simple assumptions listed in table A-1, with one additional assumption. The graph assumes that the "other costs" of the decentralized decision makers are less than those of the centralized decision makers.[3] This assumption might be true, for instance, when the decentralized decision makers are much more motivated than workers who were just following orders would be. If this assumption is not true (if the costs of decentralized decision makers are higher than the costs of centralized decision makers), then decentralized decision makers are never desirable, and the centralized region extends all the way to the vertical axis.

FIGURE A-2

Desirable Decision-Making Structures for Different Kinds of Decisions

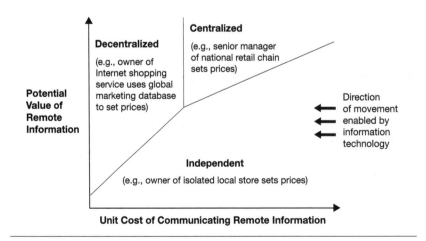

190

To understand figure A-2, consider two kinds of decisions. Decisions in which remote information is expensive to communicate relative to its value in decision making would be toward the lower right side of the figure. As the figure shows, the independent decision makers who already have the information should usually make these decisions. Even in centralized national retail chains, for instance, local store managers usually make their own decisions about whom to hire as clerks.

On the other hand, if the remote information is valuable enough, then the decision would be near the top of the figure. In this case, it may be worth paying significant communication costs to transmit the information somewhere else for decision making. For instance, basic accounting information about how much money is received and spent in each store is of significant value in making many kinds of business decisions. This information is thus nearly always communicated elsewhere, whether for centralized decision making in a single place (centralized decision makers) or decentralized decision making in multiple places (decentralized decision makers).

Information Technology and the Evolution of Centralization

Figure A-2 shows that an important effect of information technology is to reduce the costs of communicating many kinds of information. This means that, in general, we can expect a given type of decision (say, product pricing decisions) to move gradually leftward in the figure as the unit costs decline for communicating the kinds of information this type of decision uses. Thus, many decisions will pass through a stage of being centralized before eventually moving to a structure with connected, decentralized decision makers.

This figure, therefore, summarizes the logical basis for the recurring pattern of organizational changes we've seen. When communication costs are extremely high, the independent decision-making structure is the most desirable one. But as information technology reduces communication costs, many decisions will pass through a stage of having centralized decision makers before eventually moving to a structure with decentralized decision makers.

Of course, this entire progression will not always occur. For instance, when the remote information is of only moderate value (and the other costs of centralized control are high), we might see a transition from independent decision makers directly to decentralized decision makers. Instead of creating a centrally owned chain of local truck repair shops, Caterpillar, the truck engine manufacturer, developed a PC-based service that lets independent truck repair shops use a national database of repair histories for individual truck engines.[4] Similarly, in situations where the remote information is even less valuable (and the costs of connected decentralized decision making are also relatively high), then independent decision makers may be the most desirable structure even when communication costs become zero.

In general, however, we should expect decreasing communication costs to lead to movement along the path just described when (1) local decisions can be significantly improved by considering remote information, and (2) some other benefit of decentralization is also important. These other benefits, for instance, might include those listed in chapter 3:

1. Local decision makers are significantly more enthusiastic, committed, and creative when they have more autonomy in their work.

2. Local decisions can also be significantly improved by taking into account local information that is hard to communicate (i.e., "sticky").

3. Local decision makers value freedom and individualization.

Notes

Preface

1. See Thomas W. Malone, Robert J. Laubacher, and Michael S. Scott Morton, eds., *Inventing the Organizations of the 21st Century* (Cambridge, MA: MIT Press, 2003).

2. For a recent summary of work on coordination theory, see Gary M. Olson, Thomas W. Malone, and John B. Smith, eds., *Coordination Theory and Collaboration Technology* (Mahwah, NJ: Erlbaum, 2001).

3. Thomas W. Malone, JoAnne Yates, and Robert I. Benjamin, "Electronic Markets and Electronic Hierarchies," *Communications of the ACM [Association for Computing Machinery]* 30, no. 6 (1987): 484–497.

4. Thomas W. Malone, "Is 'Empowerment' Just a Fad? Control, Decision-Making, and Information Technology," *Sloan Management Review* 38, no. 2 (1997): 23–35.

Chapter 1

1. See, for example, Charles Handy, *The Age of Unreason* (Boston: Harvard Business School Press, 1990); Tom Peters, *Liberation Management* (New York: Knopf, 1992); James Brian Quinn, *Intelligent Enterprise: A Knowledge and Service Based Paradigm for Industry* (New York: Free Press, 1992); Peter F. Drucker, *Post-Capitalist Society* (New York: HarperBusiness, 1993); Kevin Kelly, *Out of Control* (Reading, MA: Addison-Wesley, 1994); Russell Ackoff, *The Democratic Corporation* (New York: Oxford University Press, 1994); Charles Handy, *The Age of Paradox* (Boston: Harvard Business School Press, 1994); John H. Holland, *Hidden Order* (Reading, MA: Addison-Wesley, 1995); Stuart Kauffman, *At Home in the Universe* (New York: Oxford University Press, 1995); Sumantra Ghoshal and Christopher A. Bartlett, *The Individualized Corporation* (New York: HarperBusiness, 1997); Dee Hock, *Birth of the Chaordic Age* (San Francisco: Berrett-Koehler, 1999); Eric Bonabeau, Marco Dorigo, and Guy Theraulaz, *Swarm Intelligence* (New York: Oxford University Press, 1999); Charles A. O'Reilly III and Jeffrey Pfeffer, *Hidden Value* (Boston: Harvard Business School Press, 2000); Don Tapscott, David Ticoll, and Alex Lowy, *Digital Capital: Harnessing the Power of Business Webs* (Boston: Harvard Business School Press, 2000); Steven Johnson, *Emergence* (New York: Scribner, 2001); Shoshana Zuboff and James Maxmin, *The Support Economy* (New York: Viking, 2002);

Peter F. Drucker, *Managing in the Next Society* (New York: Truman Talley Books/ St. Martin's Press, 2002); Brook Manville and Josiah Ober, *A Company of Citizens* (Boston: Harvard Business School Press, 2003).

2. See, for example, JoAnne Yates, *Control through Communication: The Rise of System in American Management* (Baltimore: Johns Hopkins University Press, 1989).

3. For more on the centralized mind-set, see Mitchel Resnick, *Turtles, Termites, and Traffic Jams: Explorations in Massively Parallel Microworlds* (Cambridge, MA: MIT Press, 1997).

Chapter 2

1. See, for example, Jared Diamond, *The Third Chimpanzee* (New York: Harper Collins, 1992), 36.

2. Ibid., 45.

3. Richard B. Lee and Richard Daly, eds., *The Cambridge Encyclopedia of Hunters and Gatherers* (New York: Cambridge University Press, 1999), 1–19.

4. This egalitarian decision making was apparently very common, but not universal, in hunter-gatherer societies. For a discussion of exceptions, see Robert L. Keely, "Hunter-Gatherer Economic Complexity and 'Population Pressure': A Cross-Cultural Analysis," *Journal of Anthropological Archaeology* 7 (1988): 373–411.

5. Richard B. Lee, *The !Kung San* (New York: Cambridge University Press, 1979), 343–344, quoted in *The Evolution of Human Societies: From Foraging Group to Agrarian State,* by Allen W. Johnson and Timothy Earle (Stanford, CA: Stanford University Press, 1987), 52. See also numerous related sources in Johnson and Earl, *The Evolution of Human Societies,* 39–54.

6. Ibid.

7. G. Henriksen, *Hunters in the Barrens: The Naskapi on the Edge of the White Man's World,* Newfoundland Social and Economic Studies No.12 (Newfoundland, Canada: Institute of Social and Economic Research, 1973), 42, summarized by Tim Ingold, "On the Social Relations of the Hunter-Gatherer Band," in *The Cambridge Encyclopedia of Hunters and Gatherers,* ed. Richard B. Lee and Richard Daly (New York: Cambridge University Press, 1999), 407.

8. Of course, in different places around the world, there were many differences in the specific techniques of hunting and gathering, in the size of groups, in the degree of egalitarianism, and in many other aspects of daily life. See Robert L. Kelly, *The Foraging Spectrum: Diversity in Hunter-Gatherer Lifeways* (Washington, DC: Smithsonian Institution Press, 1995), for an extensive analysis of differences among diverse hunter-gatherer groups.

9. See, for example, Jared Diamond, *Guns, Germs, and Steel* (New York: W. W. Norton, 1997), 86, 110–112, 135; J. R. Harlan, *Crops and Man,* 2nd ed. (Madi-

son, WI: American Society for Agronomy, 1992), summarized in *People of the Earth: An Introduction to World Prehistory,* 10th ed., by Brian Fagan (Upper Saddle River, NJ: Prentice Hall, 2001), 236.

10. S. E. Finer, *The History of Government from the Earliest Times,* vols. 1–3 (Oxford: Oxford University Press, 1999), 39, 112–114, 116, 139–147; Brian Fagan, *People of the Earth,* 390–402.

11. See, for example, Elman Service, *Primitive Social Organization* (New York: Random House, 1962); Elman Service, *Origins of the State and Civilization* (New York: W. W. Norton, 1975); Morton Fried, *The Evolution of Political Society* (New York: Random House, 1967); Johnson and Earle, *The Evolution of Human Societies;* Keely, "Hunter-Gatherer Economic Complexity," 404; Kelly, *The Foraging Spectrum,* 304; Diamond, *The Third Chimpanzee,* 281; Robert Wright, *Non Zero: The Logic of Human Destiny* (New York: Pantheon, 2000).

12. Diamond, *Gun, Germs, and Steel,* 215; Wright, *Non Zero,* 93.

13. Wright, *Non Zero,* 94; Diamond, *Gun, Germs, and Steel,* 215. Even the Incas, who are regarded by some (e.g., Diamond, *Gun, Germs, and Steel,* 215) as having a state-level organization without writing, apparently had an equivalent technology for record keeping and communication, based on a very complex and sophisticated system of knotted strings. See Marcia Ascher and Robert Ascher, *The Code of the Quipu* (Ann Arbor, MI: University of Michigan Press, 1981), cited and summarized in *People of the Earth,* 599.

14. Peter Farb, *Man's Rise to Civilization,* 2nd ed. (New York: E. P. Dutton, 1978), 169, cited in *Non Zero,* 32.

15. Farb, *Man's Rise to Civilization,* 180–181; Carleton S. Coon, *The Hunting Peoples* (New York: Little, Brown, & Co., 1971), 35–37, 66–67, 126–129, 134–134, 143–146, 271 (both references cited in *Non Zero,* 32).

16. Wright, *Non Zero,* 33.

17. Diamond, *The Third Chimpanzee,* 190.

18. Diamond, *Gun, Germs, and Steel,* 291–292.

19. Ibid., 289–292.

20. Ibid., 289–291.

21. Ibid., 274.

22. Ibid., 265–292.

23. Of course, humans don't always want more freedom. Human nature includes elements of both egalitarianism and hierarchy. On the one hand, our human genes evolved in a world of egalitarian bands—even today many people resist being told what to do by others. On the other hand, humans are primates, and many primates have clearly developed dominance hierarchies. For example, when male baboons in the African savanna are matched on a one-to-one basis, there is a consistent linear hierarchy of dominance across all the pairs. See Irven DeVore and Sherwood L. Washburn, "Baboon Ecology and Human Evolution," in *African Ecology and Human Evolution,* ed. F. Clark Howell and

Francois Bourliere (New York: Wenner-Gren Foundation for Anthropological Research, 1963), cited in *The Tangled Wing: Biological Constraints on the Human Spirit,* by Melvin Konner (New York: Holt, Rinehart and Winston, 1982), 39.

In general, therefore, all people have natural tendencies toward both egalitarianism and hierarchy. But the transition to hierarchical societies required most people to give up more of their freedom than they had ever had to do in all of human history up to that point.

24. See, for example, Brook Manville and Josiah Ober, *A Company of Citizens* (Boston: Harvard Business School Press, 2003).

25. Finer, *History of Government,* 322–324.

26. Ibid., 90–93, 238–241, 1024–1051, 1501–1516, 1538–1542.

27. Ibid., 1541.

28. Philip Slater and Warren G. Bennis, "Democracy Is Inevitable," *Harvard Business Review,* March–April 1964 (reprinted, with updated commentaries, September–October 1990, 167–175).

Chapter 3

1. On Nike, see Debora Spar and Jennifer Burns, "Hitting the Wall: Nike and International Labor Practices," Case no. 9-700-047 (Boston: Harvard Business School, 2000); on HP, see Molly Williams, "Hewlett-Packard Faces Sharpest Criticism of Compaq Deal from Its Own Employees," *Wall Street Journal,* 16 November 2001; on BP, see Steven E. Prokesch, "Unleashing the Power of Learning: An Interview with British Petroleum's John Browne," *Harvard Business Review,* September–October 1997.

2. Alfred D. Chandler, Jr., *The Visible Hand: The Managerial Revolution in American Business* (Cambridge, MA: Harvard University Press, 1977), 51.

3. Ibid., 51–52.

4. Ibid., 37.

5. On Phoenician traders, see, for example, M. E. Aubet, *The Phoenicians and the West: Politics, Colonies and Trade,* trans. M. Turton (Cambridge: Cambridge University Press, 1996); Karl Moore and David Lewis, *Foundations of Corporate Empire: Is History Repeating Itself?* (London: Financial Times/Prentice Hall, 2000), ch. 5, especially 50–53. On the Catholic Church, see S. Harris, "Confession-Building: Long-Distance Networks and the Organization of Jesuit Science," *Early Science and Medicine* 1, no. 3 (1996): 287–318. On the Hudson Bay Company, see Michael O'Leary, Wanda Orlikowski, and JoAnne Yates, "Distributed Work over the Centuries: Trust and Control in the Hudson Bay Company," in *Distributed Work,* ed. Pamela J. Hinds and Sara Kiesler (Cambridge, MA: MIT Press, 2002), 1670–1826.

6. Chandler, *The Visible Hand,* 107–108.

7. Ibid., 236.

8. Ibid., 280.

9. Erik Brynjolfsson, Thomas W. Malone, Vijay Gurbaxani, and Ajit Kambil, "Does Information Technology Lead to Smaller Firms?" *Management Science* 40, no. 12 (1994): 1628–1644. There is some ambiguity about what has happened to firm size since our study in the mid-1990s. See, for instance, Frederic L. Pryor, "Will Most of Us Be Working for Giant Enterprises by 2028?" *Journal of Economic Behavior and Organization* 44 (2001): 363–382.

10. "Top 500 Companies by Employees," in *Hoover's Master List of U.S. Companies 2003* (Austin, TX: Hoover's, 2002), 7. The 2,042,400 employees listed for Manpower include temporary workers, so some lists of the largest employers (e.g., *D&B Business Rankings, 2002 Edition* [Bethlehem, PA: Dun & Bradstreet, 2002]) do not list Manpower as number one.

11. See, for example, Don Tapscott, David Ticoll, and Alex Lowy, *Digital Capital: Harnessing the Power of Business Webs* (Boston: Harvard Business School Press, 2000).

12. See, for example, Elizabeth D. Scott, K. C. O'Shaughnessy, and Peter Capelli, "Management Jobs in the Insurance Industry: Organizational Deskilling and Rising Pay Inequity," in *Broken Ladders,* ed. Paul Osterman (New York: Oxford University Press, 1996), 126–154.

13. Raghuram G. Rajan and Julie Wulf, "The Flattening Firm: Evidence from Panel Data on the Changing Nature of Corporate Hierarchies" (paper presented at the National Bureau of Economic Research Conference on Organizational Economics, Cambridge, MA, 22–23 November 2002). Also available at <http://www-management.wharton.upenn.edu/wulfresearch/Papers/Flattening_Firm_11_02.pdf> (accessed 23 May 2003).

14. Erik Brynjolfsson and Lorin Hitt, "Beyond Computation: Information Technology, Organizational Transformation and Business Performance," *Journal of Economic Perspectives* (fall 2000): 23–48.

15. JoAnne Yates, *Control through Communication: The Rise of System in American Management* (Baltimore: Johns Hopkins University Press, 1989).

16. Delays and costs for one destination come directly from JoAnne Yates and Robert Benjamin, "The Past and Present As a Window on the Future," in *The Corporation of the 1990's,* ed. Michael S. Scott Morton (New York: Oxford University Press, 1991), 72. They made the following assumptions: One page of text is transmitted from New York to Chicago, approximately 850 miles. For pre-railroad and railroad delivery, the cost is the U.S. mail rate for a letter. For telegraph transmission, the page of text is assumed to be reduced to fifty billable words by means of the compression and codes typically used then. The transmission time of five minutes for telegraph includes conversion at both ends.

I made the following additional assumptions to calculate the delays and costs for one hundred destinations: The destinations are scattered around the United States, no two in the same place, but the average distance and delay for all the destinations is the same as that from New York to Chicago. The page of text to be transmitted has already been written, and in the case of e-mail, it has already been written in an electronic medium (e.g., the mail system). For mailing letters (pre-railroad and railroad), the letter must be copied by hand ninety-nine times. Copying one page of text by hand takes approximately five minutes (0.083 hour). Cost of copying a page of text by hand is $0.83 (based on a labor rate of $10.00 per hour). For telegrams, two telegraph operators are available simultaneously in the telegraph office where the message originates, so two telegrams can be transmitted simultaneously.

Other than labor rates for copying text, all costs are expressed in actual (not constant) dollars. The effects of inflation would make the contrast even more dramatic.

17. Thomas W. Malone, JoAnne Yates, and Robert I. Benjamin. "Electronic Markets and Electronic Hierarchies," *Communications of the ACM* 30, no. 5 (1987): 484–497.

18. Brynjolfsson et al., "Does Information Technology Lead to Smaller Firms?"

19. See, for example, Teresa Amabile, B. A. Hennessey, and B. S. Grossman, "Social Influences on Creativity: The Effects of Contracted-For Reward," *Journal of Personality and Social Psychology* 50 (1986): 14–23; Teresa Amabile, *Creativity in Context* (Boulder, CO: Westview Press, 1996), 176–177; Teresa Amabile, "Motivating Creativity in Organizations: On Doing What You Love and Loving What You Do," *California Management Review* 40, no. 1 (fall 1997): 48; Teresa Amabile, R. Conti, H. Coon, J. Lazenby, and M. Herron, "Assessing the Work Environment for Creativity," *Academy of Management Journal* 39, no. 5 (1996): 1154–1184.

20. Amabile, "Motivating Creativity in Organizations."

21. Albert Einstein, "Autobiography," in *Albert Einstein: Philosopher-Scientist,* ed. P. Schilpp (Evanston, IL: Library of Living Philosophers, 1949), 18.

22. See, for example, J. R. Hackman and G. Oldham, *Work Redesign* (Reading, MA: Addison-Wesley, 1980).

23. See, for example, Vijay Gurbaxani and Seungjin Whang, "The Impact of Information Systems on Organizations and Markets," *Communications of the ACM* 43, no. 1 (1991): 59–73; Paul Attewell and James Rule, "Computing and Organizations: What We Know and What We Don't Know," *Communications of the ACM* 17, no. 12 (1984): 1184–1192; Joey F. George and John L. King, "Examining the Computing and Centralization Debate," *Communications of the ACM* 34, no. 7 (1991): 63–72.

Citing examples of large or centralized organizations that continue to thrive, several recent authors have attempted to refute the argument that information technology leads to smaller or more decentralized organizations. See, for example, Francis Fukuyama, *Trust: The Social Virtues and the Creation of Prosperity*

(New York: Free Press, 1995), 24; John Seely Brown and Paul Duguid, *The So-cial Life of Information* (Boston: Harvard Business School Press, 2000), 26–31. Our model, as described in this chapter and in chapter 8, helps explain in more detail the conditions under which we should expect to see this kind of increasing centralization and those under which we wouldn't.

In one particularly intriguing article, the authors note that today's postindustrial organizations bear a striking resemblance to the protoindustrial organizations that preceded the industrial revolution (Susan J. Winter and S. Lynne Taylor, "The Role of Information Technology in the Transformation of Work: A Comparison of Postindustrial, Industrial, and Protoindustrial Organization," *Information Systems Research* 7 [March 1996]: 5–21). These authors view this observation as a surprising paradox that calls into the question the technology-based explanations of the current change. But our model provides a possible explanation for this seemingly paradoxical observation.

24. For a similar observation, see Fukuyama, *Trust,* 341.

25. More precisely, our work shows that, other things being equal, we should expect to see this sequence (independent decision makers followed by centralized decision makers followed by decentralized decision makers) when the following three conditions are present: (1) communication costs are steadily declining, (2) each stage in this sequence requires more communication than the previous one, and (3) each stage has some important advantages over the previous one.

26. In many business books, the basic logical structure is to describe a number of business case examples and then look for patterns they have in common. In this book, by contrast, the driving examples come from many millennia of human history, and the "amazing pattern" shows what these examples have in common. The business case examples presented later in the book, therefore, are not intended to prove that the pattern is happening; they are just intended to illustrate it.

Chapter 4

1. Example based on Craig Silverstein, "Google, Innovation, and the Web" (presentation at the O'Reilly Emerging Technology Conference, Santa Clara, CA, 25 April 2003). I am indebted to Jonathan Grudin for suggesting this example.

2. See "The Word Spy," <http://www.wordspy.com/words/egoboo.asp> (accessed 27 May 2003). See also the following commentary about egoboo: Robert D. Hof, "Tech Outfits Should Take Notes," *BusinessWeek,* 3 March 2003, 86.

3. For the encyclopedia itself and an extensive history and description of the site's editorial policies, see <http://www.wikipedia.org> (accessed 29 April 2003). See also Kendra Mayfield, "Not Your Father's Encyclopedia," *Wired News,*

28 January 2003 <http://www.wired.com/news/culture/0,1284,57364,00.html> (accessed 29 April 2003); Ben Hammersley, "Common Knowledge," *Guardian Unlimited,* 30 January 2003 <http://www.guardian.co.uk/online/story/0,3605,884666,00.html> (accessed 29 April 2003).

4. "Wiki software" makes it easy to create or edit hypertext documents (like those on the World Wide Web) without having to know the details of the HTML (hypertext markup language) used by most Web pages. See <http://www.wikipedia.org/wiki/Wiki> (accessed 27 April 2003).

5. Dave Brooks, "Site Makes Use of Useful, Useless Facts," *Nashua (NH) Telegraph,* 12 February 2003. Available on the Web at <http://www.nashuatelegraph.com/Main.asp?SectionID=30&SubSectionID=90&ArticleID=73632> (accessed 26 April 2003).

6. Wikipedia online encyclopedia, s.v. "Wikipedia," <www.wikipedia.org/wiki/Wikipedia> (accessed 27 April 2003). Nupedia (http://www.nupedia.com) is an open-content encyclopedia that requires peer reviewing. Many people who worked on it shifted their attention to Wikipedia, and Nupedia has been inactive since October 2001.

7. See <www.wikipedia.org/wiki/Wikipedia:Policies and guidelines> (accessed 27 April 2003).

8. From AES Corporate Web site <http://www.aes.com> (accessed 23 May 2003).

9. Suzy Wetlaufer, "Organizing for Empowerment: An Interview with AES's Roger Sant and Dennis Bakke," *Harvard Business Review,* January–February 1999, 112.

10. Carol Bowers, "The Amazing Rise of AES," *Utility Business,* April 2000.

11. Wetlaufer, "Organizing for Empowerment," 114.

12. Dennis Bakke, personal communication in meeting attended by the author, AES Headquarters, Arlington, VA, 7 August 2001.

13. Ibid.

14. Ibid.

15. Wetlaufer, "Organizing for Empowerment," 117.

16. Bakke, personal communication, 7 August 2001.

17. Wetlaufer, "Organizing for Empowerment," 120.

18. Bakke, personal communication, 7 August 2001.

Chapter 5

1. Example based on Charles Fishman, "Whole Foods Is All Teams," *Fast Company* 2 (April 1996): 103; Amy Hopfensperger (Public Relations Manager, Whole Foods Market), telephone conversation with author, 21 May 2003.

2. For an excellent introduction to the idea of democracy in business, see Brook Manville and Josiah Ober, *A Company of Citizens* (Boston: Harvard Busi-

ness School Press, 2003). For other overviews, see Charles Manz and Henry Simms, Jr., *Business Without Bosses* (New York: John Wiley & Sons, 1995); Russell Ackoff, *The Democratic Corporation* (New York: Oxford University Press, 1994); Patricia McLagan and Christo Nel, *The Age of Participation* (San Francisco: Berrett-Koehler Publishers, 1995); Ronald E. Purser and Steve Cabana, *The Self-Managing Organization* (New York: Free Press, 1998).

For other early examples of democratically managed organizations, see Polly LaBarre, "This Organization Is Dis-Organization," *Fast Company* 3 (June/July 1996): 77 (Oticon); Charles Fishman, "Engines of Democracy," *Fast Company* 28 (October 1999): 174 (General Electric jet engine plant in Durham, NC); Charles Leadbeater, *The Weightless Society* (New York and London: Texere, 2000), 68–71 (St. Luke's advertising agency).

3. Example based on author's conversation with a director of the firm, 29 September 2002. The names of the firm and the director are withheld to protect confidentiality.

4. Molly Williams, "Hewlett-Packard Faces Sharpest Criticism of Compaq Deal from Its Own Employees," *Wall Street Journal,* 16 November 2001.

5. Examples in this section are based on the following sources: Michael Kaplan, "You Have No Boss," *Fast Company* 11 (October–November 1997): 226; John Huey, "The New Post-Heroic Leadership," *Fortune,* 21 February 1994, 42–50; W. L. Gore corporate Web site, "Fast Facts," <http://www.gore.com/about/fastfacts.html> (accessed 24 May 2003); Charles C. Manz and Henry P. Sims, Jr., *Business without Bosses* (New York: John Wiley & Sons, 1995), 131–150; Rick Carter, "Quality's Different Drummer," *Industrial Maintenance and Plant Operation,* January 2002, cover story.

6. Kaplan, "You Have No Boss."

7. Ibid.

8. Alastair McCall, ed., "The Firm That Lets Staff Breathe," *Sunday Times* (London), 24 March 2002, (in "One Hundred Best Companies to Work For" special section).

9. Dee Hock, *Birth of the Chaordic Age* (San Francisco: Berrett-Koehler, 1999), 103, 106–111, 161, 181–185, 189–190.

10. Visa International corporate Web site, "About Visa," <http://corporate.visa.com/av/main.shtml> (accessed 24 May 2003).

11. Robert D. Hof, "The People's Company: eBay Is Run Like a Democracy, with Customers Playing a Major Role. But Will That Relationship Become a Casualty of the Auction Site's Success?" *BusinessWeek,* 3 December 2001, 15–21.

12. Mary Lou Song, quoted in Jason Black, "Lean on Me: Companies on the Web Are Learning That Paying Attention to Users Who Call the Shots Makes Good Sense for Business," *Internet World,* 15 May 2001.

13. Ibid.

14. Ibid.

15. Statistics from eBay Company Update, May 2003 <http://www.share holder.com/ebay/downloads/StandardPresentation051203a.pdf> (accessed 25 May 2003).

16. See Mondragon corporate Web site, <http://www.mondragon.mcc.es> (accessed 16 September 2002) and Mondragon Cooperative Corporation Corporate Profile (brochure) 2001. Some details about Mondragon in the following paragraphs are also based on conversations with Mondragon managers (27–28 June 2002) and subsequent personal communications. Iñaki Dorronsoro, R&D Centers and Mondragon University Coordinator, was especially helpful in clarifying several issues.

17. Russell Ackoff, *The Democratic Corporation* (New York: Oxford University Press, 1994), 110–141, describes a somewhat similar idea, which he calls a "circular organization." In a circular organization, all managers at all levels of the organization have their own boards. These boards include the manager's supervisor and all the manager's direct subordinates. Thus, all managers, in some sense, report to their subordinates.

18. On disproportionate pay for executives, see Jennifer Gill, "We're Back to Serfs and Royalty," *BusinessWeek Online,* 9 April 2001, available at <http://www.businessweek.com/careers/content/apr2001/ca2001049_100.htm>. Gill quantified the salary chasm between chief executives and their workers: "CEOs at 365 of the largest public companies . . . averaged $13.1 million in 2000, roughly 531 times more than their average employees."

19. See the following Web site of the National Center for Employee Ownership (NCEO), <http://www.nceo.org/library/eo100.html> (accessed 15 August 2002). The companies named here are the three largest on a list compiled in July 2002 by NCEO. Companies on the list must be at least 50 percent owned by employees through an employee ownership plan in which most or all full-time employees can participate, unless employee groups are excluded by collective bargaining agreements.

20. David Wooley, "Introduction to a New Corporate Structure (1983)," posting on the Global Ideas Bank Web site, <http://www.globalideasbank.org/inspir/INS-57.HTML> (accessed 30 May 2003) and at <http://thinkofit.com/drwool/newcorps.htm> (accessed 30 May 2003); Robert Laubacher, Thomas W. Malone, and The 21st Century Scenario Working Group, "Two Scenarios for 21st Century Organizations: Shifting Networks of Small Firms or All-Encompassing 'Virtual Countries'?" in *Inventing the Organizations of the 21st Century,* ed. Thomas W. Malone, Robert J. Laubacher, and Michael S. Scott Morton (Cambridge, MA: MIT Press, 2003).

21. A particularly intriguing generalization of this scenario is what might be called a proxy democracy. In a proxy democracy, you can exercise your right to

vote by giving someone else your proxy—the right to vote on your behalf on a certain set of issues. And anyone who has your proxy can, in turn, delegate it further. In the scenario described in the text, your manager automatically has your proxy for all issues on which you don't vote yourself.

But there is no reason, in principle, why you couldn't give your proxies to a variety of other people besides your manager for different issues. For instance, you might give your proxy for hiring decisions to one person and your proxy for budget decisions to someone else. Then the person who has your proxy for budget decisions might further transfer your proxy to one person for budgets in Division A and to someone else for budgets in Division B. And, if you don't like the ways these people are voting on your behalf, you can always transfer your proxies to someone else or vote directly yourself.

In general, a proxy democracy solves the same basic problem a representative democracy does: It lets people express their general preferences without having to take the time to vote on every issue. But a proxy democracy solves this problem in a much more flexible and powerful way: You don't have to spend any more time on issues than you want to, but when you care about an issue, you can have much more direct influence than just writing to your elected representative.

Although no place that I know of has tried a proxy democracy, it seems to be eminently worth trying—both in government and in business. Like many other possibilities described in this book, this idea is much more feasible with cheap and convenient communication technology.

22. Dennis Bakke, personal communication, 7 August 2001.

23. In 2001–2002, virtually the entire energy industry, including AES, suffered significant stock price declines, but this seems to reflect more on the energy business than on how AES is organized.

Chapter 6

1. Thomas W. Malone and Robert J. Laubacher, "The Dawn of the E-lance Economy," *Harvard Business Review,* September–October 1998, 144–152.

2. The following statistical summary of this issue is based on work by my colleague Rob Laubacher: U.S. Bureau of Labor Statistics (BLS) Household Survey for April 2003 indicates that out of 137.7 million working Americans, 24.4 million were part-timers (17.7 percent) and 10.1 million (7.3 percent) were self-employed. This gives a total of 34.5 million workers (25.0 percent) who are self-employed or part-time. The BLS Establishment Survey also indicates that in the same month, 2.7 million Americans were employed as temporary workers in the help-supply services industry. Some of these workers are presumably already counted as part-timers in the Household Survey. Assuming

that the proportion of part-time workers is the same in this industry as in the economy as a whole, however, we can estimate that approximately 5 million of the temporary workers were part-timers, leaving approximately 2.3 million full-time temporary workers (1.6 percent of the workforce). Adding all these types of nontraditional workers together, approximately 26.7 percent of the U.S. workforce is either part-time, temporary, or self-employed. See U. S. Department of Labor, Bureau of Labor Statistics Data, <http://www.bls.gov/data/home.htm> (accessed 29 May 2003).

3. Thomas W. Malone, JoAnne Yates, and Robert I. Benjamin. "Electronic Markets and Electronic Hierarchies," *Communications of the ACM* 30, no. 6 (1987): 484–497.

4. For a discussion of some difficulties of balancing freelance or self-employed work with family responsibilities, see, for example, Meg Lundstrom, "The New Mommy Track: Chief Executive, Cook, and Bottle Washer," *Business-Week Online,* 2 December 1999, <http://www.businessweek.com/smallbiz/9912/f991202.htm> (accessed 27 May 2003).

5. The founders of this company used as their company name the word we coined in our *Harvard Business Review* article. Later, I became a member of the firm's advisory board.

6. Statistics from "eBay Company Update, May 2003" <http://www.shareholder.com/ebay/downloads/StandardPresentation051203a.pdf> (accessed 25 May 2003), and Melanie Warner, "eBay's Worst Nightmare," *Fortune,* 26 May 2003, 89–94.

7. "Ebay Offers Health Insurance for Some," *Boston Globe,* 8 January 2003.

8. "Top 500 Companies by Employees," *Hoover's MasterList of U.S. Companies 2003* (Austin, TX: Hoover's, 2002), 7. At 150,000 employees, eBay would be tied with Blue Cross Blue Shield (number 36) between United Technologies (35) and PepsiCo (37).

9. For a sophisticated analysis of how and why eBay's reputation mechanism works, see Chrysanthos Dellarocas, "Efficiency and Robustness of eBay-like Online Reputation Mechanisms in Environments with Moral Hazard," working paper 170, MIT Center for eBusiness, Cambridge, MA, 2003.

10. Robert D. Hof, "The People's Company: eBay Is Run Like a Democracy, with Customers Playing a Major Role. But Will That Relationship Become a Casualty of the Auction Site's Success?" *BusinessWeek* 3 (December 2001): 15–21. By comparison, credit card fraud is nine times as high as the eBay rate. For an alternative interpretation, suggesting that actual fraud may be somewhat higher than reported on eBay, see Warner, "eBay's Worst Nightmare," 90.

11. The following discussion on guilds is based on Rober J. Laubacher and Thomas W. Malone, "Flexible Work Arrangements and 21st Century Worker's Guilds," working paper 004, MIT Initiative on Inventing the Organizations of

the 21st Century, Boston, October 1997; Thomas W. Malone and Robert J. Laubacher, "The Rebirth of the Guild," *Boston Globe,* 24 August 2000; Thomas W. Malone and Robert J. Laubacher, "Retreat of the Firm and the Rise of Guilds: The Employment Relationship in an Age of Virtual Business," in *Inventing the Organizations of the 21st Century,* ed. Thomas W. Malone, Robert J. Laubacher, and Michael S. Scott Morton (Cambridge, MA: MIT Press, 2003).

12. Paul Osterman et al., *Working in America: A Blueprint for the New Labor Market* (Cambridge, MA: MIT Press, 2001).

13. Steven Greenhouse, "The Most Innovative Figure in Silicon Valley? Maybe This Labor Organizer," *New York Times,* 14 November 1999.

14. "Ebay Offers Health Insurance for Some," *Boston Globe,* 8 January 2003.

Chapter 7

1. Ajit Kambil and Eric van Heck, *Making Markets: How Firms Can Design and Profit from Online Auctions and Exchanges* (Boston: Harvard Business School Press, 2002), 127–128, 160; Jeff Morgheim, statement to the U.S. Senate Committee on Commerce, Science, and Transportation, 21 September 2000, available at <http://www.gcrio.org/OnLnDoc/pdf/pdf/morgheim000921.pdf> (accessed 6 June 2003); British Petroleum corporate Web site, "Our Performance," <http://www.bp.com/environ_social/environment/climate_change/our_performance/index.asp#10> (accessed 12 March 2003).

2. For a classic overview of transfer pricing, see Robert J. Eccles, *The Transfer Pricing Problem: A Theory for Practice* (Lexington, MA: Lexington Books, 1985). For a more recent description of several innovative versions of this approach, see Russell Ackoff, *The Democratic Corporation* (New York: Oxford University Press, 1994), 142–167.

3. AnnaLee Saxenian, *Regional Advantage: Culture and Competition in Silicon Valley and Route 128* (Cambridge, MA: Harvard University Press, 1994).

4. John Byrne, "The Miracle Company: Excellence in the Lab and Executive Suite Makes Merck a Powerhouse," *BusinessWeek,* 19 October 1987, 86.

5. Robert J. Laubacher and Thomas W. Malone, "Temporary Assignments and a Permanent Home: A Case Study in the Transition to Project-Based Organizational Practices," working paper, MIT Center for Coordination Science, Cambridge, MA, 2003. I am especially indebted to Rob Oyung of Hewlett-Packard for bringing this example to our attention and for his insightful help during the project.

6. C. R. Plott, "Markets as Information Gathering Tools," *Southern Economic Journal* 67, no. 1 (2000): 1–15; Kay-Yut Chen and Charles R. Plott, "Prediction Markets and Information Aggregation Mechanism: Experiments and Application," technical report, California Institute of Technology, Pasadena, CA, 1998. The name of the company is not identified in these reports, but it is identified

in several other references to them, e.g., Hal R. Varian, "Effect of the Internet on Financial Markets," technical report, School of Information Management and Systems, University of California, Berkeley, September 1998; Robin Hanson, "Shall We Vote on Values, but Bet on Beliefs?" technical report, Department of Economics, George Mason University, Fairfax, VA, September 2000, available at <http://hanson.gmu.edu/futarchy.pdf> (accessed 6 June 2003).

7. The prices and other information generated by a market like this might be used to calculate an even more accurate prediction of the future than the market itself makes. See Kay-Yut Chen, Leslie R. Fine, and Bernardo A. Huberman, "Forecasting Uncertain Events with Small Groups," in Proceedings of the ACM Conference on E-commerce, Tampa, FL, October 2001.

8. See the list of publications about idea futures on Robin Hanson's Web site, <http://hanson.gmu.edu/ideafutures.html> (accessed 6 June 2003).

9. "Iowa Electronic Markets," <http://www.biz.uiowa.edu/iem/> (accessed 6 June 2003).

10. Robert Forsythe et al., "Anatomy of an Experimental Political Stock Market," *American Economic Review* 85, no. 5 (1992): 1142–1161.

11. Ibid.; R. Forsythe, T. Rietz, and T. Ross, "Wishes, Expectations and Actions: A Survey on Price Formation in Election Stock Markets," *Journal of Economic Behavior and Organization* 39, no. 1 (1999): 83–110.

12. Nicholas Chan, Ely Dahan, Adlar Kim, Andrew Lo, and Tomaso Poggio, "Securities Trading of Concepts (STOC)," working paper 172, MIT Center for eBusiness, Cambridge, MA, December 2002.

13. Shailagh Murray, "Online Exchange Chooses Turmoil As a Commodity," *Wall Street Journal,* 29 July 2003; Peter Coy, "Betting on Terror: PR Disaster, Intriguing Idea," *BusinessWeek,* 25 August 2003, 41; Jeremy Kahn, "The Man Who Would Have Us Bet on Terrorism—Not to Mention Discard Democracy and Cryogenically Freeze Our Heads—May Have a Point (About the Betting, We Mean)," *Fortune,* 15 September 2003, 179–186.

The original proposal was widely condemned because it might have allowed terrorists to profit from their misdeeds and because some felt it was immoral to bet on things like murder and destruction in the first place. Insurance companies, however, wager on people's lives every day, and trading on certain kinds of particularly objectionable events (like assassinations of specific individuals) could easily have been prohibited in the market. In addition, since gains were limited to $100, no one could have profited substantially anyway. One particularly promising variation of the idea would have been to open the market only to invited experts from government, academia, and industry. This could have created a kind of expert consensus for predicting danger much more efficiently than conventional means.

14. See detailed examples and references in Hanson, "Shall We Vote on Values?" 12–13.

15. The other MIT researchers involved in this project included Jim Rice, David McAdams, Adlar Kim, Jim Hines, John Quimby, George Herman, Ben Koo, and Paulo Gonçalves.

16. The number one hundred is chosen arbitrarily here for illustration; it does not reflect the actual value in use at the company. A wafer is a thin sheet of silicon that may contain hundreds or thousands of individual integrated circuits.

17. Adlar Kim customized this system for our use. For more details on the basic system, see Chan et al., "Securities Trading of Concepts (STOC)."

18. See, for example, Ronald Coase, "The Nature of the Firm," *Econometrica* 4 (1937): 386–405; Oliver Williamson, *Markets and Hierarchies: Analysis and Antitrust Implications* (New York: Free Press, 1975); Oliver Williamson, *Economic Institutions of Capitalism* (New York: Free Press, 1985); Oliver Williamson, *The Mechanisms of Governance* (New York: Oxford University Press, 1996); Sanford Grossman and Oliver Hart, "The Costs and Benefits of Ownership: A Theory of Vertical and Lateral Integration," *Journal of Political Economy* 94 (1986): 691–719; Oliver Hart and John Moore, "Property Rights and the Nature of the Firm," *Journal of Political Economy* 27 (1990): 1119–1158; Bengt Holmstrom and Paul Milgrom, "Multitask Principal-Agent Analyses: Incentive Contracts, Asset Ownership, and Job Design," *Journal of Law, Economics, and Organization* 7 (1991): 24–52; Robert Gibbons, "Taking Coase Seriously," *Administrative Science Quarterly* 44 (1999): 145–157; Bengt Holmstrom and John Roberts, "The Boundaries of the Firm Revisited," *Journal of Economic Perspectives* 12, no. 4 (1998): 73–94.

19. Charles H. Fine, *Clockspeed* (New York: Perseus, 1999).

Chapter 8

1. Louis V. Gerstner, Jr., *Who Says Elephants Can't Dance? Inside IBM's Historic Turnaround* (New York: HarperBusiness, 2002), 12–13, 57–62, 68–70.

2. Ibid., 22.

3. Ibid., 248–252.

4. For related work that contributed to the development of this approach, see Jay R. Galbraith, *Designing Organizations: An Executive Guide to Strategy, Structure, and Process,* 2nd ed. (San Francisco: Jossey-Bass, 2002); K. A. Merchant, "The Control Function of Management," *Sloan Management Review* 23, no. 4 (spring 1982): 43–55.

5. On the growing importance of knowledge work, see, for example, Peter F. Drucker, *Post-Capitalist Society* (New York: HarperBusiness, 1993).

6. Thomas W. Malone, "Is 'Empowerment' Just a Fad? Control, Decision-Making, and Information Technology," *Sloan Management Review* 38, no. 2 (1997): 23–35; M. Stevenson, "The Store to End All Stores," *Canadian Business Review,* May 1994; B. Fox, "Staying on Top at Wal-Mart," *Chain Store Age*

Executive 70, no. 4 (1994): 47; Thomas Richman, "Mrs. Fields' Secret Ingredient," *INC. Magazine,* October 1987, 65–72.

7. Merchant, "The Control Function of Management."

8. See, for example, Chrysanthos Dellarocas, "The Digitization of Word-of-Mouth: Promise and Challenges of Online Reputation Mechanisms," working paper, MIT Sloan School of Management, Cambridge, MA, 2002; Paul Resnick et al., "Reputation Systems," *Communications of the ACM* 43, no. 12 (2000): 45–48.

9. Capital One Financial Corporation, "Securities and Exchange Commission Form 8-K," 16 July 2002, available at <http://www.sec.gov/Archives/edgar/data/927628/000092838502002514/d8k.htm> (accessed 2 June 2003).

10. Brent Schlender, "Intel's $10 Billion Gamble," *Fortune,* 11 November 2002, 90.

11. Goran Lindahl, conversation with author, Carmel, CA, 24 June 2001.

12. Rebecca Smith, "AES, Calpine Post Losses for the Quarter: Results Reflect Electric-Power Industry's Tight Credit, Instability, Declining Margins," *Wall Street Journal,* 14 February 2003.

13. Stephanie Woerner, "Networked at Cisco," Case SeeIT #1 (Cambridge, MA: MIT Sloan School of Management SeeIT Project Working Paper), 2001.

14. Paul Milgrom and John Roberts, "The Economics of Modern Manufacturing: Technology, Strategy, and Organization," *American Economic Review* 80, no. 3 (1990): 511–528; Erik Brynjolfsson, Amy Renshaw, and Marshall VanAlstyne, "The Matrix of Change: A Tool for Business Process Reengineering," *Sloan Management Review* 38, no. 2 (winter 1997): 37–54.

15. Charles A. O'Reilly III and Jeffrey Pfeffer, *Hidden Value: How Great Companies Achieve Extraordinary Results with Ordinary People* (Boston: Harvard Business School Press, 2000), 222–226.

16. See, for example, Edgar Schein, *Process Consultation: Lessons for Managers and Consultants,* vol. 1 (2nd ed.) and vol. 2 (Reading, MA: Addison Wesley, 1987 and 1988); Tracy Goss, Richard Tanner Pascale, and Anthony G. Athos, "The Reinvention Roller Coaster: Risking the Present for a Powerful Future," *Harvard Business Review,* November–December 1993, 97–108; John P. Kotter, *Leading Change* (Boston: Harvard Business School Press, 1996); John P. Kotter and Dan S. Cohen, *The Heart of Change: Real Life Stories of How People Change Their Organizations* (Boston: Harvard Business School Press, 1996); Jim Collins, *Good to Great: Why Some Companies Make the Leap . . . and Others Don't* (New York: HarperCollins, 2001).

17. I am indebted to Rob Laubacher for suggesting and explaining this example to me. For background, see Michael Storper and Susan Christopherson, "Flexible Specialization and Regional Industrial Agglomerations: The Case of the U.S. Motion Picture Industry," *Annals of the Association of American Geographers* 77, no. 1 (1987), 104–117.

Chapter 9

1. For previous uses of the term *orchestrator* in this same sense, see John Hagel III, Scott Durchslag, and John Seely Brown, "Loosening Up: How Process Networks Unlock the Power of Specialization," *McKinsey Quarterly*, 31 May 2002, 59–69; John Hagel III, *Out of the Box: Strategies for Achieving Profits Today and Growth Tomorrow through Web Services* (Boston: Harvard Business School Press, 2002), 114–116.

2. Douglas Ready, "Mobilizing Collective Ambition: How Effective Top Teams Lead Enterprise-Wide Change," working paper, International Consortium for Executive Development Research, Lexington, MA, July 2002.

3. I am indebted to Don Lessard for a discussion that helped clarify the points in this section.

4. See, for example, the following Web sites: "The Apache Software Foundation," <http://www.apache.org>; "The Apache XML Project: Project Guidelines," <http://xml.apache.org/guidelines.html>; "The Apache Jakarta Project," <http://jakarta.apache.org/site/guidelines.html> (all accessed 8 June 2003).

5. Robert J. Herbold, "Inside Microsoft: Balancing Creativity and Discipline," *Harvard Business Review*, January 2002, 73–79.

6. Rebecca M. Henderson and Kim B. Clark, "Architectural Innovation: The Reconfiguration of Existing Product Technologies and the Failure of Established Firms," *Administrative Science Quarterly* 35 (1990): 9–30.

7. Klaus-Dieter Heerklotz (Manager, IT and Multimedia Services, VIAG Interkom), conversation with author, Monte Carlo, Monaco, 8 June 1999.

8. Hagel, *Out of the Box;* John Hagel III and John Seely Brown, "Your Next IT Strategy," *Harvard Business Review*, October 2001, 105–113.

9. F. Warren McFarlan and Fred Young, "Li & Fung: Internet Issues (A)," Case 9-301-009 (Boston: Harvard Business School, 2000).

10. For an example of a framework from which such shared electronic activity maps might emerge, see Thomas W. Malone, Kevin G. Crowston, and George Herman, eds., *Organizing Business Knowledge: The MIT Process Handbook* (Cambridge, MA: MIT Press, 2003).

11. Hagel, Durchslag, and Brown, "Loosening Up: How Process Networks Unlock the Power of Specialization."

12. Thomas W. Malone and Kevin Crowston, "The Interdisciplinary Study of Coordination," *ACM Computing Surveys* 26, no. 1 (1994): 87–119.

13. See, for example, Gary M. Olson, Thomas W. Malone, and John B. Smith, eds., *Coordination Theory and Collaboration Technology* (Mahwah, NJ: Erlbaum, 2001).

14. Kevin Crowston, "Towards a Coordination Cookbook: Recipes for Multi-Agent Action" (Ph.D. diss., MIT Sloan School of Management, 1991); Gilad

Zlotkin, "Coordinating Resource Based Dependencies," working paper (unpublished), Center for Coordination Science, MIT, Cambridge, MA, 1995; Thomas W. Malone et al., "Tools for Inventing Organizations: Toward a Handbook of Organizational Processes," *Management Science* 45, no. 3 (1999): 425–443.

15. Thomas W. Malone, "How Can You Systematically Invent New Business Ideas? Leveraging an Online Process Handbook," working paper, MIT Center for Coordination Science, Cambridge, MA, 2003.

16. For much more detailed descriptions, see Malone et al., "Tools for Inventing Organizations"; Malone, Crowston, and Herman, eds., *Organizing Business Knowledge*. The results of our MIT research have also been commercialized by Phios Corporation (www.phios.com), an MIT spin-off company of which I am cofounder and chairman.

17. For more detail, see George Herman and Thomas W. Malone, "What Is in the Process Handbook? An Overview of Its Contents," in *Organizing Business Knowledge: The MIT Process Handbook,* ed. Thomas W. Malone, Kevin G. Crowston, and George Herman (Cambridge, MA: MIT Press, 2003).

18. Malone et al., "Tools for Inventing Organizations."

Chapter 10

1. See, for example, Charles Handy, *The Age of Unreason* (Boston: Harvard Business School Press, 1990); Tom Peters, *Liberation Management* (New York: Knopf, 1992); Charles Handy, *The Age of Paradox* (Boston: Harvard Business School Press, 1994); Russell Ackoff, *The Democratic Corporation* (New York: Oxford University Press, 1994); Charles Manz and Henry Simms, Jr., *Business without Bosses* (New York: John Wiley & Sons, 1995); Patricia McLagan and Christo Nel, *The Age of Participation* (San Francisco: Berrett-Koehler, 1995); Sumantra Ghoshal and Christopher A. Bartlett, *The Individualized Corporation* (New York: HarperBusiness, 1997); Ronald E. Purser and Steve Cabana, *The Self-Managing Organization* (New York: Free Press, 1998); Dee Hock, *Birth of the Chaordic Age* (San Francisco: Berrett-Koehler, 1999); Charles A. O'Reilly III and Jeffrey Pfeffer, *Hidden Value* (Boston: Harvard Business School Press, 2000).

2. Linda Seger and Edward Jay Whetmore, *From Script to Screen: The Collaborative Art of Filmmaking* (New York: Henry Holt & Co., 1994), 72.

3. Ibid., 97.

4. Dwight Eisenhower, quoted in *American Speaker,* ed. Aram Bakshian, Jr. (Washington, D.C.: Georgetown Publishing House, 1994), QUO/23.

5. Alexandre Ledru-Rollin, quoted in *American Speaker,* QUO/22.

6. Mike Linksvayer, "The Choice of a Gnu Generation: An Interview with Linus Torvalds," *Meta* (online magazine), 12 November 1993, <http://gondwanaland.com/meta/history/interview.html> (accessed 1 June 2003).

7. Philip Elmer-Dewitt, "Why Java Is Hot," *Time,* 22 January 1996, 58–60.

8. Mao Tse-tung, speech given in Peking, 27 February 1957, in *Selected Works of Mao Tse-tung* (Peking, Foreign Languages Press, 1977), 408.

9. Richard Foster and Sarah Kaplan, *Creative Destruction: Why Companies That Are Built to Last Underperform the Market—and How to Successfully Transform Them* (New York: Doubleday/Currency, 2001).

10. Wanda J. Orlikowski, "Learning from Notes: Organizational Issues in Groupware Implementation," in *Proceedings of the Third ACM Conference on Computer-Supported Cooperative Work* (Toronto, November 1992), 362–369.

11. Wanda J. Orlikowski and J. Debra Hofman, "An Improvisational Model of Change Management: The Case of Groupware Technologies," *Sloan Management Review* 38, no. 2 (winter 1997): 11–21. I have substituted the term *opportunistic* for these authors' original term: *opportunity-based.*

12. Jim Collins, *Good to Great* (New York: HarperBusiness, 2001), 17–40.

13. Deborah Ancona, Thomas W. Malone, Wanda Orlikowski, and Peter Senge, "Core Capabilities of Distributed Leadership," working paper, MIT Sloan School of Management, Cambridge, MA, forthcoming. The following four sections (on the four capabilities) are based on this paper and on other material developed jointly by the authors of this working paper.

14. The complete (initially confidential) memo is now available as exhibit 20 in the Microsoft antitrust trial: <http://www.usdoj.gov/atr/cases/exhibits/20.pdf> (accessed 1 June 2003).

15. Don Meichenbaum, "Enhancing Creativity By Modifying What Subjects Say to Themselves," *American Educational Research Journal* 12 (1975): 132, cited in *Creativity in Context,* by Teresa Amabile (Boulder, CO: Westview Press, 1996), 247).

16. See, for example, reviews and summaries of a number of techniques in M. I. Stein, *Stimulating Creativity,* vols. 1 and 2 (New York: Academic Press, 1974 and 1975); L. Rose and H. Lin, "A Meta-Analysis of Long-Term Creativity Training Programs," *Journal of Creative Behavior* 18 (1984): 11–22; Amabile, *Creativity in Context.*

17. See, for example, Alex F. Osborne, *Applied Imagination: Principles and Procedures of Creative Thinking* (New York: Scribner's, 1963).

18. Thomas W. Malone, "How Can You Systematically Invent New Business Ideas? Leveraging an On-line Process Handbook," working paper, MIT Center for Coordination Science, Cambridge, MA, 2003.

19. Mark Granovetter, "The Strength of Weak Ties," *American Journal of Sociology* 78 (1973): 1360–1380.

20. Deborah Ancona, Henrik Bresman, and Katrin Kaeufer, "The Comparative Advantage of X-Teams," *Sloan Management Review* 43, no. 3 (spring 2002): 33–39.

Chapter 11

1. This version is adapted from Stephen R. Covey, *The 7 Habits of Highly Effective People* (New York: Simon & Schuster, 1990), 95–144.

2. See, for example Frederick F. Reichheld, *The Loyalty Effect: The Hidden Force behind Growth, Profits, and Lasting Value* (Boston: Harvard Business School Press, 1996); Frederick F. Reichheld, *Loyalty Rules! How Leaders Build Lasting Relationships* (Boston: Harvard Business School Press, 2001).

3. MIT 21st Century Manifesto Working Group (Deborah Ancona, Lotte Bailyn, Erik Brynjolfsson, John Carroll, Tom Kochan, Don Lessard, Thomas W. Malone [chair], Wanda Orlikowski, Jack Rockart, Michael S. Scott Morton, Peter Senge, John Sterman, and JoAnne Yates), "What Do We Really Want? A Manifesto for the Organizations of the 21st Century," in *Inventing the Organizations of the 21st Century,* ed. Thomas W. Malone, Robert J. Laubacher, and Michael S. Scott Morton (Cambridge, MA: MIT Press, 2003). Also available at <http://ccs.mit.edu/papers/pdf/wp032manifesto21C.pdf> (accessed 11 June 2003).

4. See, for instance, A. H. Maslow, *Motivation and Personality,* 3rd ed. (New York: Harper & Row, 1987); E. E. Lawler, *Motivation in Work Organizations* (San Francisco: Jossey-Bass,1994). Maslow's original theory was that your needs at one level are active only when your needs at all the levels below it have been satisfied. Later research has found little evidence that Maslow's exact groupings and sequence are correct, but it does seem that some needs don't become important until others are satisfied. For instance, Lawler (*Motivation in Work Organizations,* ch. 2) found evidence of a two-level grouping (like the one described here), with higher-level needs (such as love, esteem, and self-actualization) being satisfied in any order only after physiological and safety needs were met.

5. Business Roundtable, *Statement on Corporate Responsibility* (New York, 1981), 9; Business Roundtable, *Statement of Corporate Governance* (New York, 1997), 3. (Both cited and summarized in "Beyond Selfishness," by Henry Mintzberg, Robert Simons, and Kunal Basu, *Sloan Management Review* 44, no. 1 (2002): 67–74.)

6. Milton Friedman, "The Social Responsibility of Business Is to Increase Its Profits," *New York Times Magazine,* 13 September 1970, 32–33, 122–126.

7. The claim that corporations can have nonfinancial goals is true, not just philosophically, but also legally. In the United States, for instance, corporate officers are generally legally allowed to do what is in the best interests of the corporation, broadly conceived. For example, the Massachusetts General Laws, Part I, Title XII, Chapter 156B, Section 65, says: "In determining what he reasonably believes to be in the best interests of the corporation, a director may consider the interests of the corporation's employees, suppliers, creditors and customers, the economy of the state, region and nation, community and societal considerations, and the long- term and short-term interests of the corpora-

tion and its stockholders, including the possibility that these interests may be best served by the continued independence of the corporation."

8. For further information, see, for instance, the following Web sites: <http://www.socialinvest.org> and <http://www.betterworld.com> (both accessed 15 May 2002).

9. See, for instance, Jason Zweig, "What Would Jesus Buy?" *Time,* 19 May 2003, 86.

10. Social Investment Forum, *2001 Report on Socially Responsible Investing Trends in the United States* (Washington, DC: Social Investment Forum, 2001), <http://www.socialinvest.org/Areas/research/trends/SRI_Trends_Report_2001.pdf> (accessed 13 June 2003).

11. Suzy Wetlaufer, "Organizing for Empowerment: An Interview with AES's Roger Sant and Dennis Bakke," *Harvard Business Review,* January–February 1999, 112.

12. For an insightful commentary on the issues in this section, see Charles Handy, "What's a Business For?" *Harvard Business Review,* December 2002, 49–55.

13. Zweig, "What Would Jesus Buy?"

14. See, for example, British Petroleum's corporate Web site at <http://www.bp.com/index.asp> (accessed 1 July 2003).

15. Michael Skapinker, "Why Nike Has Broken Into a Sweat," *Financial Times* (FT.com), 6 March 2002, available at <http://news.ft.com/ft/gx.cgi/ftc?pagename=View&c=Article&cid=FT363BTGHYC&live=true> (accessed 7 May 2002).

16. Peter Dizikes, "Analyze This: In Terror Fight, CIA Leans on Analysts to See Big Picture," ABCNews.com, 10 June 2002, <http://abcnews.go.com/sections/business/DailyNews/ciaagents020610.html> (accessed 1 July 2003).

17. Enron Corporation, "Code of Ethics," (Houston: Enron Corporation, 2000), <http://www.thesmokinggun.com/enron/enronethics1.shtml> (accessed 13 June 2003).

18. London Greenpeace, "What's Wrong with the Body Shop? A Criticism of 'Green' Consumerism," (London: London Greenpeace, 1998), <http://www.mcspotlight.org/beyond/companies/bs_ref.html> (accessed 13 June 2003).

19. See, for example, the Web site of the Global Reporting Initiative, <http://www.globalreporting.org/index.htm>, (accessed 7 October 2002).

20. "About ratings," IdealsWork corporate Web site, <http://www.idealswork.com/ratings/index.asp#1> (accessed 7 September 2003).

21. Comparison done in October 2002.

22. Idries Shah, *A Perfumed Scorpion* (London: Octagon Press, 1978), 140–141.

23. Aldous Huxley, *The Perennial Philosophy* (1944; reprint, New York: HarperCollins, 1990, Perennial Library edition), uses the name the *perennial philosophy* for this common core of religious and spiritual teachings throughout

the ages. For similar collections illustrating commonalities across different religions, see Robert Cecil, ed., *The King's Son* (London: Octagon Press, 1981); Dorothy B. Phillips, Elizabeth B. Howes, and Lucille M. Nixon, eds., *The Choice Is Always Ours* (San Francisco: Harper, 1975).

24. E. F. Schumacher, *Small Is Beautiful* (London: Blond & Briggs Ltd, 1973; New York: Harper Perennial, 1989), 318.

Appendix

1. For a more detailed description of this model, see Thomas W. Malone, "Is 'Empowerment' Just a Fad? Control, Decision-Making, and Information Technology," *Sloan Management Review* 38, no. 2 (1997): 23–35; George M. Wyner and Thomas W. Malone, "Cowboys or Commanders: Does Information Technology Lead to Decentralization?" *Proceedings of the International Conference on Information Systems (ICIS 96)* (Cleveland, OH, 15–18 December 1996).

2. See, for example, Paul J. DiMaggio and Walter W. Powell, "The Iron Cage Revisited: Institutional Isomorphism and Collective Rationality in Organizational Field," *American Sociological Review* 48 (1983): 147–160; Jay R. Galbraith, *Organization Design* (Reading, MA: Addison-Wesley, 1977); Vijay Gurbaxani and Seungjin Whang, "The Impact of Information Systems on Organizations and Markets," *Communications of the ACM* 34, no. 1 (1991): 59–73; George P. Huber and Reuben R. McDaniel, "The Decision-Making Paradigm of Organizational Design," *Management Science* 32, no. 5 (1986): 572–589; M. Lynne Markus, "Power, Politics, and MIS Implementation," *Communications of the ACM* 26, no. 6 (1983): 430–444; Edgar H. Schein, *Organizational Culture and Leadership* (San Francisco: Jossey-Bass, 1985); W. Richard Scott, *Organizations: Rational, Natural, and Open Systems,* 3rd ed. (Englewood Cliffs, NJ: Prentice-Hall, 1992); J. D. Thompson, *Organizations in Action* (New York: McGraw-Hill, 1967).

3. The mathematical proof of this result is given in Wyner and Malone, "Cowboys or Commanders." A similar model with essentially identical results was developed independently at Stanford University: Namhoon Kwon, "Three Essays on the Theory of the Firm" (Ph.D. diss., Department of Economics, Stanford University, 1997): 1–46.

4. D. Sullivan, "On the Road Again," *CIO Magazine,* 15 January 1995, 50–52.

Index

About the Author

Thomas W. Malone is the Patrick J. McGovern Professor of Management at the MIT Sloan School of Management. He is also the founder and director of the MIT Center for Coordination Science and was one of the two founding codirectors of the MIT Initiative "Inventing the Organizations of the 21st Century."

Professor Malone teaches classes on leadership and information technology, and his research focuses on how new organizations can be designed to take advantage of the possibilities provided by information technology. In an article published in 1987, for example, Professor Malone predicted many of the major developments in electronic business in the 1990s: electronic buying and selling, electronic markets for many kinds of products, the outsourcing of noncore functions in a firm, and the use of intelligent agents for commerce.

Professor Malone has published two *Harvard Business Review* articles and more than fifty research papers and book chapters; he is an inventor with eleven patents; and he is the coeditor of three books: *Coordination Theory and Collaboration Technology* (Erlbaum, 2001), *Inventing the Organizations of the 21st Century* (MIT Press, 2003), and *Organizing Business Knowledge: The MIT Process Handbook* (MIT Press, 2003).

Malone has been a cofounder of three software companies and has consulted and served as a board member for a number of other organizations. Before joining the MIT faculty in 1983, he was a research scientist at the Xerox Palo Alto Research Center (PARC), where his research involved designing educational software and office information systems. His background includes a Ph.D. and two master's degrees from Stanford University, a B.A. (magna cum laude) from Rice University, and degrees in applied mathematics, engineering-economic systems, and psychology.